# India's Strategic Thought
# *and*
# Multi-Domain Perspectives

# India's Strategic Thought *and* Multi-Domain Perspectives


*Editors*

Maj Gen Sanjeev Chowdhry (Retd)

Komal Chaudhary

Vinayak Sharma


United Service Institution of India

Army War College


PENTAGON PRESS LLP

First published in 2024 by

PENTAGON PRESS LLP
206, Peacock Lane, Shahpur Jat
New Delhi-110049, India
Contact: 011-26490600

Printed by Aegean Offset Printers, Noida

ISBN 978-81-971986-2-5



**www.pentagonpress.in**

# Contents

# Foreword

In an era marked by rapid geopolitical shifts and evolving security challenges, the examination of strategic thought and the adaptation of military doctrine become imperative endeavours for any nation. As the complexities of modern warfare continue to expand across multiple domains, the need for insightful analysis and strategic foresight becomes ever more critical.

The United Service Institution of India (USI) and the Army War College (AWC) have collaborated on a seminal joint publication, focusing on strategic thought and multi-domain warfare capabilities of India. This collaborative effort represents a significant milestone in the scholarly exploration of India's strategic landscape and its preparedness to confront the challenges of contemporary warfare.

India's strategic thought is deeply rooted in its rich history, cultural heritage, and geopolitical realities. As a nation with diverse strategic interests and a commitment to regional stability, India's approach to warfare encompasses a comprehensive understanding of both traditional and non-traditional domains. We are witnessing multi-domain warfare and grey-zone conflicts across the spectrum of conflicts and up the escalation ladder. These developments merit a serious reflection and debate. The analysis explores the profound influence of spiritual beliefs on Indian strategic thought, investigating how these beliefs have formed political ideology, military strategy and interstate relations. This publication delves into India's strategic thought steeped in its ancient scriptures and philosophy by delving into ancient texts like the *Adnyapatra* (Royal Edict), during the era of Chhatrapati Shivaji Maharaj and the timeless wisdom of Thiruvalluvar's *Thirukkural* (Sacred Verses), which advocates for a whole-of-nation approach to rediscover and revive India's ancient heritage, while celebrating the rich legacy of the Ahom dynasty in Northeast India, showcasing their military prowess, administrative innovation, and cultural inclusivity as testament to India's diverse historical tapestry and strategic heritage.

The articles compiled within this book offer a comprehensive exploration of multi-domain operations, spanning from their historical foundations to contemporary challenges and their strategic implications, with a particular emphasis on the Indian context. They illuminate the significance of innovation, collaboration, and adaptability in navigating the intricacies of modern warfare in the 21st Century. Delving into the emergence of grey zone operations, the text unveils their strategic nuances and enduring relevance, drawing insights from India's rich military history and strategic doctrines like *Kootneeti* (Strategy) from Kautilya's *Arthashastra* (Economics). Moreover, the publication examines the pivotal role of technology-driven victories, the rise of Unmanned Aircraft Systems (UAS), and the imperative for counter-UAS capabilities in today's military landscape. It also delves into the concept of electromagnetic manoeuvre warfare, emphasising agility and dominance within the electromagnetic spectrum environment. Addressing the role of air power in grey zone operations and the growing prevalence of such activities in the maritime domain, particularly China's, the text underscores the necessity for effective mechanisms to manage these challenges without resorting to outright conflict. Finally, it highlights the complexities of holding actors accountable in the ambiguous realm of grey zone activities, advocating for enhancements to international legal frameworks and conflict management mechanisms.

Moreover, this joint publication serves as a testament to the enduring partnership between the USI and AWC. By fostering intellectual exchange and collaboration, both institutions contribute towards the advancement of strategic studies and the development of future leaders in the field of national security.

I am sanguine that this publication will serve as a valuable resource for scholars, policymakers, and military professionals seeking to deepen their understanding of India's strategic thought and its implications for multi-domain warfare. May it inspire further research and debate among strategic analysts.

**Major General BK Sharma AVSM, SM****
***Director General, United Service Institution of India***

# Message

The world order today is a complex canvas with conflicts, contests and competition in the geopolitical, military, economic and diplomatic realms. Norms of international behaviour and lessons of the past have been fractured with the third year of the Russia-Ukraine conflict, breaching of perceived perfect intelligence grid of Israel riding on technology and human assets, ultimate deception executed by Hamas on 07 Oct 2023 and thereafter winning the information warfare narrative. The holy grail of allowing free and safe movements for sea faring mercantile has been shattered not by pirates but by nation states and non-state actors. The world has never been as much in flux as it is today. The strategicians are surely at sea to understand the complexities of the contemporary world environment, unable to crystal gaze the emerging future alignments, challenges and opportunities and create solutions for crisis after crisis impacting the humanity.

On the other hand, warfighting, riding the overhang of rapidly emerging technology in this conundrum, has become more complex, warranting an in-depth understanding of Multi-domain Warfare, which is being prosecuted by nations and non-state actors both in times of war and peace.

It is with this background, the inaugural edition of Joint USI-AWC Publication was conceived on two themes 'India's Strategic Thought and Multi-domain Perspectives'. This is the third collaborative project between AWC and USI in past two years, other two being '*Shaurya Sankalan*: Digital Archiving of History of Indian Army' and publication of a military history book 'Valour and Honour'. The sharing of this inaugural edition will enlighten and empower the scholar warriors with India's strategic thought and multi-domain perspectives.

The AWC and USI, have a reputation for publishing journals and publications of strategic direction. I am sanguine that this collaborative joint effort on two contemporary themes consisting of well researched and thought provoking articles will provide valuable inputs to the readers.

I take this opportunity to compliment both the editorial teams for selecting relevant articles from a wide pool and putting forth a highly professional publication on a contemporary subject.

Happy Reading

Jai Hind

**Lieutenant General DP Pandey, PVSM, UYSM, AVSM, VSM**
***Commandant, Army War College***

# The Publication at a Glance

We are proud to present a joint publication brought to you by the United Service Institution of India (USI) and the Army War College (AWC). This collaborative effort aims to offer comprehensive insights into the complexities of India's strategic thought, and contemporary multi-domain operations and grey zone warfare drawing from a diverse range of perspectives and expertise.

The first section of this joint publication delves into India's strategic thought, tracing its evolution from ancient scriptures and historical figures like Chanakya to contemporary foreign policy. It highlights the core principle of '*Vasudhaiva Kutumbakam*' (The World is One Family) and concepts like '*Viksit Bharat*' (Developed India) and '*Atmnirbhar Bharat*' (Self-reliant India), rooted in India's civilisational wisdom. The publication analyses the influence of spiritual beliefs on political ideology, military strategy, and inter-state relations, while addressing contemporary challenges like regional instability and cyber threats. It explores the concept of strategic culture and examines historical texts like *Adnyapatra* (Royal Edict) to refine India's strategic outlook for the future, emphasising critical analysis and drawing parallels with modern strategic concepts. Thiuvalluvar's *Thirukkural* (Sacred Verses), dating back nearly 2,000 years, reveals profound wisdom that requires a whole-of-nation approach and revival of ancient teachings, considering the perils of dynastic rule and historical invasions that have threatened India's cultural inheritance. Finally, it underscores the legacy of the Ahom dynasty in the Northeast India, showcasing their military prowess and cultural inclusivity as integral parts of India's rich historical and strategic heritage.

The second section of the publication focuses on Multi-Domain Operations (MDO) as a critical aspect of modern warfare, exploring its theoretical foundations, practical applications, and challenges within the Indian context. It analyses real-world case studies like the Russia-Ukraine War, to understand how MDO strategies are utilised to achieve strategic objectives. Additionally, it addresses India's operational and strategic hurdles in implementing MDO and advocates for proactive measures to adapt to 21$^{st}$ Century security challenges. This section also delves into grey zone tactics and India's military heritage, emphasising timeless strategic principles and the disruptive impact of technologies like Unmanned Aircraft Systems (UAS), counter-UAS operations and electro-magnetic manoeuvre warfare. Furthermore, it examines the role of air power and maritime aspects to explore plausible options to address evolving security threats, concluding with insights into the military applications of Open Artificial Intelligence's Generative Pre-trained Transformer-4 and the challenges posed by the grey zone conflict for international law enforcement.

This joint publication offers a comprehensive exploration of India's strategic thought and its approach to MDO, addressing the complex challenges of the 21$^{st}$ Century through collaborative research and inter-disciplinary analysis. We express our sincere gratitude to the Commandant of the AWC and the Director-General of the USI for their visionary leadership in conceiving this annual joint publication, which fosters collaboration and knowledge sharing, advancing strategic discourses and enhancing understanding of contemporary security challenges.

***The Editorial Team***
**Major General Sanjeev Chowdhry (Retd)**
**Ms Komal Chaudhary**
**Mr Vinayak Sharma**

# List of Contributors

*Major General BK Sharma, AVSM, SM** (Retd)* is the Director General of USI of India. He specialises in strategic net assessment, scenario building, and strategic gaming.

*Lieutenant General DP Pandey, PVSM, UYSM, AVSM, VSM* is the Commandant, Army War College. He was commissioned into the 9th (th in superscript do not print) Battalion, the Sikh Light Infantry Regiment. Throughout his career, he held various command and staff roles in diverse terrains and operational settings. Notably, he participated in Op VIJAY (Kargil) in 1999 and commanded his unit in Siachen Glacier and Eastern Ladakh. Later, he commanded a Rashtriya Rifles Sector and a Counter Insurgency Force in Kashmir. Before heading the Army War College, he served as the General Officer Commanding of the esteemed Chinar Corps. Additionally, he was the inaugural Director General of the Territorial Army. He holds post graduate degrees from the Defence Services Staff College, Wellington, the National War College in Washington DC, and an MPhil from the National Defence College, New Delhi.

*Colonel Amit S Parolekar*, an Infantry officer, has served in diverse field and peace assignments. His experience includes counter insurgency/counter terrorism, high altitude areas in both Northern and Eastern Commands, and the plains and deserts on the Western Front. Apart from regimental duties, he has instructed at a Category A establishment and served as a General Staff Officer-1 in an active brigade on the Line of Control. Additionally, he worked as a Strategic Advisor to the Force Commander in Mission in the Democratic Republic of Congo. He has completed numerous certified courses on various United Nations and recently attended the Higher Command Course. Notably, he is a researcher on Shivaji and has authored several articles on the warrior in the current academic year.

*Brigadier D Seshasai Murty, SC, SM*** was commissioned in the Jat Regiment in Dec 1991. He has exposure to all operations and terrains and has excelled in line of control and counter insurgency (CI) operations. A graduate of Defence Services Staff College and Higher Command Course, he also holds an MBA in Finance. He has commanded his Battalion in CI operations, has been an Instructor Class B at Indian Army Training Team Lao PDR, General Staff Officer-1 (Operations) in a mountain brigade, and Director (Intelligence, Operations and Plans) in Defence Intelligence Agency.

*Colonel Jyotisman Hazarika* was commissioned into 10 Garhwal Rifles and later transitioned to Army Aviation. He possesses extensive experience in diverse terrains and has served as General Staff Officer-1 in the Military Operations Directorate. Colonel Hazarika has commanded two flights on the Northern Borders and an Army Aviation Squadron in the Southern Theatre. A graduate of the National Defence Academy, Defence Services Staff College, Army War College (AWC), and College of Defence Management, he is currently posted at AWC.

*Major General Sandeep S Sharda, SM, VSM* a second-generation Infantry Officer, was commissioned into the Dogra Regiment in Dec 1991. With an MSc in Defence Studies from Madras University and a Master of Management Studies from Osmania University, he has held various staff and command roles across the country. The General officer has commanded an Infantry Battalion in United Nations Interim Force in Lebanon, an Assam Rifles Sector, and a critical Sub Area along the Western Borders. He served as an Instructor at the Indian Military Academy, and the Infantry School. Awarded the Vishisht Seva Medal in 2020 and the Sena Medal in 2022, he currently serves as the Dean of Army War College, Mhow.

*Colonel Kunal Sharma* was commissioned into the Intelligence Corps in Jun 2002. An alumnus of Defence Services Staff College, he has been an Instructor Class A in Military Intelligence School and Depot, Pune. He has tenanted the appointment of General Staff Officer-1 (Operations) in a field formation and commanded an Intelligence Unit in J&K. The Officer has attended the prestigious Higher Command Course and Intelligence Staff Officers Course. He is presently posted in Faculty of Studies, Army War College.

*Colonel Apratim Sharma* belongs to the Army Air Defence (AAD) and is an alumnus of National Defence Academy, Defence Services Staff College, and Higher Command Course. He has tenanted Grade-2 staff at an Infantry Brigade in counter insurgency and along the line of actual control; Grade-1 staff at Integrated Headquarters of Ministry of Defence (Army) and commanded a specialist unit under Military Intelligence Directorate. The officer is currently posted as Colonel General Staff (AAD) at Faculty of Studies and Leadership, Army War College. He is an adventure sports enthusiast.

*Colonel Nirbhay Gautam* is an Armoured Corps Officer who has experience serving in varied terrains along Northern and Western Borders. An alumnus of Defence Services Staff College and Higher Defence Management Course, the officer has tenanted staff and instructional appointments, including General Staff Officer-1 of a mountain brigade, Chief Operations Officer with the Special Representative of the Secretary-General Secretariat at United Nations Organisation Stabilisation Mission in the Democratic Republic of the Congo, Director T-90 at Directorate General Armoured Corps, and Platoon Commander at Indian Military Academy. He has commanded an Armoured Regiment in the desert and obstacle-ridden terrain along Western Borders. He is currently tenanting the appointment of Colonel General Staff(Armour) at Faculty of Studies, Army War College.

*Air Marshal Anil Khosla, PVSM, AVSM, VM* retired as the Vice Chief of the Air Staff in Apr 2019. A fighter pilot, he wields the pen with equal adeptness as he can wield the joystick. He holds two MPhil degrees on Defence and Strategic Studies and is currently pursuing a PhD on China. An ardent blogger (Air Marshal's Perspective) and Sudoku player, he has pursued the latter 10 times up to the national level.

*Captain (IN) Sarabjeet S Parmar (Retd)* is a Distinguished Fellow at the Centre for Military History and Conflict Studies at the United Service Institution of India, New Delhi, and at the Council of Strategic and Defence Research, New Delhi.

*Brigadier Pawan Bhardwaj, YSM (Retd)* is an Infantry Officer with 31 years of experience. He is a Senior Research Fellow at United Service Institution of India and is researching on employment of Artificial Intelligence at the tactical level. His reading interests include technology trends, information warfare and military training.

*Mr Mohamed Zaid* was a Research Intern with United Service Institution of India. A budding scholar and a keen learner, he has special interest in niche technologies with special focus on Artificial Intelligence and its applications. He is attending Engineering Under Graduate programme at USA.

*Wing Commander (Dr) UC Jha (Retd)* has extensive field and academic experience in International Humanitarian Law, Military Law and Human Rights Law. He was awarded PhD in 'Law and Governance' by Jawaharlal Nehru University, New Delhi in 2007. His work comprises 26 books and over 120 articles published in various journals and newspapers.

# Section 1

## *India's Strategic Thought*

# 1

# Evolution of India's Strategic Thought

**Major General BK Sharma, AVSM, SM** (Retd)**

**Abstract**

*Strategic thought is a synthesis of a country's historical experience blended with contemporary geopolitics and is is fundamental for effective decision-making in various domains, influenced by Volatility, Uncertainty, Complexity, and Ambiguity (VUCA). Being a civilisational State, India is endowed with a profound strategic thought that encapsulates the wisdom of contained in our ancient scriptures and collective wisdom our sagacious leaders. The very idea of Viksit Bharat* (Developed India), *Atmanirbhar Bharat* (Self-reliant India), *India's Strategic autonomy and multi-vector foreign policy emanate from the continuum of India's strategic culture. The cultural ethos of India, rooted in principles like 'Vasudhaiva Kutumbakam' (The World is One Family), shapes its approach to international relations, emphasising peaceful coexistence and diplomacy. This article explores the evolution of India's strategic thought, drawing insights from ancient scriptures, historical figures like Chanakya, and contemporary foreign policy.*

## Introduction

Strategic thought lies at the heart of effective decision-making, whether in the realm of business, politics, or warfare. It entails a deep understanding of the geopolitics in a Volatility, Uncertainty, Complexity, and Ambiguity (VUCA) world. Geopolitics in broad terms is a relationship of geography, resources, demography, culture, ideology, and political system of a nation state that determines its international relations. Likewise, culture is a blend of a nation's core values, beliefs, traditions, patterns of behaviour, habits, symbols, achievements and particular ways of adapting to the strategic environment. In a country with robust strategic ethos, strategists must be able to step back, consider multiple perspectives, and think through the potential consequences of various courses of action. This often necessitates the ability to deal with critical uncertainties, disruptions and discontinuities. Essential elements of strategic thought are ability to take a 360-degree view, adopt critical/out of box thinking and creativity. The most effective strategies often emerge from the ability to think outside the box, to challenge conventional wisdom, and to devise innovative solutions. Strategists must be willing to question assumptions and explore unconventional approaches. Strategic thought is not a static process; it must be continuously refined and adapted in response to changing circumstances. Effective strategists are adept at monitoring the environment, gathering and analysing relevant data, and making timely adjustments to their plans.

George Tanham's work on India's strategic culture provides valuable insights into the historical and cultural factors that have shaped India's approach to national security and strategy. Tanham, an American scholar, published his seminal essay 'Indian Strategic Thought: An Interpretive Essay' in 1992, which examined the unique characteristics of India's strategic thinking and behaviour. He argued that India's strategic culture has been predominantly defensive in nature; rooted in India's historical experience of repeated invasions and the need to safeguard its civilisation. The Gandhian principles of *Ahimsa* (Non-violence) reflects in India's defence and foreign policy. Many Indian strategic analysts find Tanham's observations shallow and lacking in understanding of India's ancient wisdom. They argue that India has a very well evolved strategic culture rooted in its rich civilisational ethos, customs and traditions. No wonder that India has not only preserved its civilisational values but has evolved into a major power well–placed to play an important role in global geopolitics.

This article seeks to delve into evolution of India's strategic thought from the ancient times to the present era of *Viksit Bharat* @2047 (Developed India).

## Genesis of India's Strategic Thought

India's strategic thought is guided by the ancient philosophy of '*Vasudhaiva Kutumbakam*' (The Word is One Family); a phrase found in ancient Sanskrit scripture '*Maha Upanishad*' implying that the 'World is one family'. India's culture of forging friendships and partnerships greatly influences its foreign policy. By leveraging its soft power, historical connections, diaspora engagement, and commitment to peacekeeping, the concept of '*Atithi Devo Bhava*' (The guest is equivalent to God), emphasises the importance of hospitality and treating strangers with kindness and respect. It is this spirit that provided space for various religions to bloom in India concurrently. India is well respected for its benign and principled foreign policy. In essence, it is a civilisational state that draws immensely from its ancient wisdom. The ancient scriptures of '*Vedas*' present a comprehensive worldview that emphasises the interconnectedness of all beings and the harmonious functioning of the universe. They outline the concept of '*Rita*' or cosmic order, reflecting the balance and interdependence of the natural and moral laws. The '*Puranas*', another series of ancient scriptures provide insights into ancient customs, rituals, art forms, and social structures, giving a glimpse into the rich cultural heritage of ancient India. The '*Upanishads*' recognise the fundamental unity of all religions and spiritual paths. They promote tolerance, respect, and inclusivity towards all religious and spiritual traditions. The '*Ramayana*', a hugely popular epic, celebrates the virtues of righteousness, loyalty, courage, and selflessness. The '*Mahabharata*' another Sanskrit epic, is a classic narrative of statecraft. It explores themes such as *Dharma* (Righteousness), *Karma* (Action and its consequences), duty, loyalty, honour, sacrifice, love, and the pursuit of truth. It emphasises that violence should be the last resort and highlights the significance of diplomacy and peaceful resolutions. The widely revered book the '*Bhagavad Gita*' is an ultimate treatise of statecraft that encompasses moral, socio-political, economic, intelligence, diplomatic and cognitive domains. It is a guide to understand duty as a warrior and fight for justice. Lord Krishna in the thick of a raging battle sermonises the great warrior Arjuna with these words, "I am a warrior; defending my Nation is my *dharma*. I will train my mind, body and spirit to fight, excel in all devices and weapons of war, present and future, always protect the weak, be truthful and forthright, be humane, cultured and compassionate, fight and embrace the consequences willingly. God, give me strength that I ask nothing of you." The Gita explains the significance of controlling one's mind and senses through meditation and yoga.[1]

More significantly, India's strategic culture is shaped by a well–known statesman *Kautalya* (Chanakya), who lived during the Mauryan Empire, around the 4th Century BCE. His *Chanakya Neeti* (policy) is a collection of guidelines that cover, strategic planning, diplomacy, decision making, governance, economics, morality, and code of conduct. Taking a cue from the Chanakya thought, Nehru in the Constituent Assembly on 04 Dec 1947, said "Talking about foreign policies, the House must remember that these are not just empty struggles on a chess board; behind them lie all manner of things; ultimately, the foreign policy is the outcome of economic policy, and until India has properly evolved from her economic policy, her foreign policy will be rather vague, rather inchoate, and will be groping."[2]

The Chanakya's *Arthashastra* (Economics) is another ancient Indian treatise on statecraft and military strategy.[3] To understand its cultural impact on Indian statecraft and foreign policy, study of *Kautalya's Saptang* theory (Seven Limbed Theory) is essential. It depicts seven essential elements of a state for developing comprehensive national power and its strategic configuration for achieving national interests. These are the ruler, council of ministers, boundaries, defensive layout, economy, defence forces and alliances. Forming strategic alliances with neighbouring states is important for the state's security and prosperity. These alliances can provide support during conflicts and help in maintaining a favourable geopolitical environment.

The '*Mandala*' (Circles) Theory[4] is another significant concept mentioned in *Arthashastra* that influences India's foreign policy. It posits that the political landscape is divided into concentric circles, known as mandalas. The central state is surrounded by other states, each with its own interests and ambitions. The *Mandala* Theory highlights the dynamic nature of inter-state relationships and the need for strategic thinking and diplomacy. It suggests that the central state should focus on building alliances, assessing threats, neutralising potential adversaries, and maintaining a favourable geopolitical environment to ensure its own security and power. The relationships between these states can be categorised into four types based on their proximity to the central state:

- **Allies**. States that share a friendly relationship and common interests with the central state are considered allies. These alliances can be formal or informal and are formed to counter common threats or to pursue common goals.

- **Enemies**. States that pose a direct threat or oppose the interests of the central state are considered enemies. The central state should be wary of these states and adopt measures to defend against their aggression.

- **Allies or Enemies**. These states are located in proximity to either allies or enemies of the central state. The central state should assess their intentions and take appropriate actions to neutralise any potential threats.

- **Neutral or Indifferent States**. These states do not pose an immediate threat or have significant alliances with the central state. They are considered neutral or indifferent, and the central state should actively maintain diplomatic relations with them to prevent any potential hostility.

Chanakya further propounded the concept of '*Saam* (Persuasion), *Daam* (Rewards to allies and coercion to adversaries), *Dand* (Punishment) *Bhed* (Division)'. The *Saam, Daam, Dand, Bhed* concept provides strategies for a ruler to maintain control, manage conflicts, and protect interests. These approaches are rooted in the understanding of human nature, power dynamics, and the necessity of adapting strategies according to the specific circumstances and challenges faced by the ruler.[5]

## India's Contemporary Statecraft

Suffice it to say that India's culture plays a significant role in shaping its foreign policy. India employs soft power, such as music, dance, literature, yoga, and cuisine to promote its image abroad. Indian cinema has a massive global appeal. Its doctrine of *Ahimsa* has influenced her foreign policy approach. India played a crucial role in the Non-Aligned Movement during the Cold War, advocating for peaceful coexistence, independence, and development among nations. It is a large diaspora community around the world, estimated to be over 30 million people, who have a profound impact on its foreign policy. The historical connections with neighbouring countries, particularly in Southeast Asia, have shaped its foreign policy. The spread of Indian religions like Buddhism and Hinduism, along with cultural exchanges, have established enduring ties that influence India's approach to regional cooperation and diplomacy. India's commitment to peacekeeping efforts under the United Nations (UN) flag demonstrates its cultural values of compassion, peace, and harmony. The Indian Council for Cultural Relations plays a crucial role in organising cultural festivals, promoting educational scholarships, and facilitating cultural exchanges to foster goodwill, understanding, and friendship between nations. In sum, India is a brand name of unity in diversity; a melting pot of civilisations amalgamated seamlessly through cultural soft power. The political system with certain adaptations can serve as model for several multi-ethnic societies.

The universal appeal of the concept 'One Earth, One Family, One Future' promoted by India during the Group of 20 summit is well established. India's contemporary foreign policy is essentially formed by the vision of *Viksit Bharat*, articulated by Prime Minister Modi. It represents India's ambitious vision to transform the nation into a developed entity by the centenary of its independence in 2047. It seeks comprehensive national development complemented by credible deterrence in a multipolar world. The operative guidelines for the accomplishment of the aforesaid vision are enunciated in the form of epithets such as National Ambition and Regional Aspiration (NARA), '*Sabka Saath-Sabka Vikas, Sabka Vishwas-Sabka Prayas*'[6] (Participative Inclusive Growth), Security And Growth for All in the Region (SAGAR),[7] Digital India and *Atmanirbhar Bharat* (Self-reliant India). India is adherent of five principles of *Panchseel* (Sovereignty, Non-aggression, Non-interference, Equality and Peaceful Coexistence). India is a staunch proponent of rule based, non-hegemonic and multipolar world order. It is against joining any blocks or military alliances, advocates free access to global commons, non-discriminatory policies towards trade and technology, non-militarisation of space and unilateral imposition of models of governance. It has mooted the initiatives of International Solar Alliance, International Yoga Day and Coalition of Disaster Resilient Infrastructure. It champions the cause of Global South and reforms in the UN and other international organisations making them more representative, inclusive and effective. It has shown firm commitment to meet the obligations towards 'Climate Change', by striving to become 'Climate Neutral' by 2070.

As far as defence and security, India has a rich experience of deterring and fighting wars, participate in out-of-area contingencies (Sri Lanka and Maldives), being the third largest troop contributor for UN Peacekeeping operations and an active participant in high availability disaster recovery missions. As part of Vision *Viksit Bharat*@2047, *Atmanirbhar Bharat* has become one of the principal goals. Since independence, India been a highly import-dependent country as far as defence equipment is concerned. This dependency on imports has become a strategic vulnerability. India is developing an ecosystem that combines start-ups, Micro, Small, and Medium Enterprises (MSMEs), defence manufacturing units and private industry besides establishing two Defence Industrial Corridors in Uttar Pradesh and Tamil Nadu. India has signed an agreement with the United States (US) on critical and emerging technologies. Similar tie-ups are being mooted with European countries. The government has allowed an increase of foreign direct investment in the defence sector, on the condition that 60.0 per cent of the components in defence platforms are indigenous, ensuring that local companies receive most of the contracts. The government has taken initiatives that will encourage the private sector to develop pan-India test facilities for the private sector. There is facilitation for intellectual property, and imports and exports. The goal is to make India the net exporter worth USD 5.0 bn of defence equipment. Private industries are encouraged to invest in Research and Development (R&D). There is focus on delicensing and deregulation of the industry in its entire life cycle. The government has started the 'Innovation for Defence Excellence' initiative to nurture innovative defence sector start-ups and MSMEs.

There are pathbreaking initiatives afoot to enhance India's deterrence and war fighting capabilities in an era of collusive hybrid wars and grey zone conflicts. Concerted efforts are being made to scale up own R&D and manufacturing capabilities, improve border infrastructure and bring about technological transformation of the Armed forces. After the appointment of Chief of Defence Staff and setting up Department of Military Affairs, renewed focus is accorded to civil-military fusion, theaterisation and reforms in national security system and defence planning process. Integrated capacity development programmes are receiving utmost attention.

## Conclusion

India in essence is a civilisational state with very rich strategic culture and military heritage. Indian philosophy is an amalgamation of wisdom contained in the ancient scriptures, customs and traditions. No wonder then, Indian civilisation has survived centuries of subjugation and rejuvenated itself into a vibrant and pluralistic state, enjoying a respectable place in the comity of nations. It has protected its sovereignty and way of life despite many wars and acts of terrorism. The country today is on a fast trajectory of growth to emerge as the third largest economy in the world. It has the fourth largest military in the world and its multi-vector foreign policy has led to India emerging as a champion of Global South and an important player in shaping a multi–polar world order. In sum, India is endowed with rich strategic culture that is sophisticated, nuanced and nimble-footed, well poised to serve India's national interests.

## End Notes

1 Rajya Sabha, Unstarred Question No. 42, Answered on 18th July, 2022, https://pqars.nic.in/annex/257/AU42.pdf

2 Quoted in Sanjaya Baru, Strategic Consequences of India's Economic, Performance (New Delhi: Academic Foundation, 2006)

3 R.P. Kangle, The Kautiliya Arthasastra, Part 3 (Delhi: Motilal Banarsidass, 1965)

[4] Amalendu Misra, Rajamandala Theory and India's International Relations, IDN, Lisbon, Seminar on India's Foreign Policy and Strategic Culture (24th November 2015)

[5] Vinay Vittal, Kautilya's Arthashastra: A Timeless Grand Strategy, School of Advanced Air and Space Studies, Maxwell Air Force Base, Alabama, June 2011

[6] PM Addresses at Constitution Day Celebrations organized by Supreme Court, https://pib.gov.in/PressReleaseIframePage.aspx?PRID=1775388 accessed on 15 April 2024

[7] Maritime Cooperation With Regional Partners, https://pib.gov.in/PressReleasePage.aspx?PRID=1807607

# 2

# Overview on Indian Strategic Thought

**Lieutenant General DP Pandey, PVSM, UYSM, AVSM, VSM**

"क्षमा शोभती उस भुजंग को जिसके पास गरल हो,
उसको क्या जो दंतहीन, विषरहित, विनीत, सरल हो।"

—रामधारी सिंह "दिनकर"

**Abstract**

*This paper delves into the historical development of Indian strategic thought, uncovering its origins in ancient civilisations and charting its evolution across distinct historical epochs. It dissects the core principles that have underpinned Indian strategic thinking, such as the concept of a righteous war, non-alignment, and the armed forces' obligation to safeguard national sovereignty. The analysis explores the profound influence of spiritual beliefs on Indian strategic thought, investigating how these beliefs have formed political ideology, military strategy, and interstate relations. It further examines how strategic thought has been reshaped to confront contemporary challenges like intensifying competition between major powers, regional instability, and the growing threat of cyberattacks. Looking forward, the article outlines the emerging contours of India's contemporary strategic thought.*

## Introduction

India's strategic thought has traversed a remarkable journey, deeply intertwined with its historical, cultural, and geopolitical milieu. Rooted in millennia-old civilisation, India's strategic ethos has weathered foreign invasions, colonial domination, and the arduous path to independence. The country's strategic narrative is a tapestry woven from diverse threads of ancient wisdom, colonial experience, and contemporary imperatives. This article aims to delve into the intricate layers of India's strategic thought, unravelling its core principles, historical antecedents, and contemporary manifestations.

## The Markers of Indian Strategic Thought

The fountainhead of Indian thought on statecraft can be traced back to the *Vedic* times when the kings had no standing armies. Indian spiritual-philosophic traditions can be described in different ages, dating back to the Harappan civilisation[1] as given out in succeeding paragraphs. A basic tenet of ancient Indian political thought across the different ages was the belief that the king must regard himself not as the creator of law but only as its guardian.

- ***Vedic* Age**. As per the *Rig-Veda* (Royal Veda), the earliest (4000-2000 BCE) surviving work of literature; each tribe during this period was headed by a leader called *Rajah* (King). The *Rajah* was not considered divine nor was he an absolute monarch. Two tribal assemblies, one a small council of the great men of the tribe and the other a larger gathering of the heads of families, approved his accession to office and advised him on important matters. The democratic principles taking root in India can be traced to more than 2,500 years ago.
- ***Brahmanical* Age**. The *Brahmanical* age (2000 to 1000 BCE) is associated with rituals and certain religious practices in order to control the population with their religious interpretations. The inhabitants were known warriors and the 'Art of War' started developing from this period onwards.
- ***Upanishadic* Age**. The third period, the *Upanishadic* age (1500 to 500 BCE) was a major period during which, the *Vedanta* [2](Vedas end) was composed, which represented a psychological interpretation of the *Samhitas* (Hymns/Vedas) and were overtly critical of the notion that the performance

of religious rituals could lead to spiritual liberation.[3] There was a change in the mental mode during this period[4], when the 'Age of Intuition' started giving way to the 'Age of Reason'.

- **Epic Age**. During the fourth period, which was the Epic age (500 to 200 BCE), the great epics, *Ramayana, Mahabharata,* and its sub-epic the *Bhagavad Gita* were composed. The *Mahabharata* contains passages that dwell on the warrior's joy of battle as they fight for glory and booty. The epics address every human emotion and behaviour and are a historical account of that period which gives an insight into the political order, statecraft, and nature of warfare during this age. This was also the time when *Karma Yoga* (The yoga of action) was popularised as a path to spiritual liberation through *Dharmic* (morally upright) living.[5]

- **Classical Yogic Age**. The Classical Age refers to the period when much of the Indian subcontinent was reunited under the Gupta Empire.[6] This period is called the golden age of India and was marked by extensive achievements in science, technology, engineering, art, dialectic, literature, logic, mathematics, astronomy, religion, and philosophy that crystallised the elements of what is generally known as Hindu culture. During this age Jainism and Buddhism originated.

- **Late Classical Age**. The Late Classical Age in India began after the end of the Gupta Empire and the collapse of the Empire of Harsha in 7th Century CE. This was the beginning and end of the Kannauj kingdom, Chalukya dynasty, Cholas regime and Delhi Sultanate. After the Gupta period, a succession of powerful dynasties and empires thus came to being and some were challenged by lesser Indian rulers who also struggled for land and power through warring, until the arrival of British who colonised India during the 19th Century. The development of statecraft and art of war during this period is well documented.

- **Modern Age**. The Modern age begins with British rule in India (circa 1700 CE) and continues to the present day.

## Development of the Indian Philosophical Way

Three major contributions of ancient India, amongst many others, towards development of a strategic thought in India were the concepts of 'Sovereignty and Responsibility' of the armed forces, 'Just and Righteous War' and lastly 'Non-alignment'. India enjoyed a state system with nascent notions of constitutionalism and sovereignty nearly two millennia before the Westphalian state system evolved in Europe. While the Western Just War Theory can be divided into two main parts – Jus ad bellum (right to go to war) and Jus in bello (right conduct in war). The traditional Indian Theory of Just War also included a third aspect – going to war for a righteous cause that gave the leaders a moral high ground to wage war for the larger good. There is presence of a strong moral principle that leaders must abide by in order to gain and maintain political legitimacy in The Hindu Just War Theory. While the Doctrine of Neutrality developed in the West only after the 18$^{th}$ Century, there is abundant evidence that at least in *Vedic* and *Mauryan* times the conception was well known in ancient India. Non-alignment is direct and natural fallout of this Doctrine of Neutrality.

Philosophy shapes the overall culture and strategic thought process. Is there an Indian philosophical thought? Has it changed over the centuries? Ancient Indian political and military thought must be understood in the context of spiritual beliefs. Spiritual belief contained in Indian scriptures has influenced the psychological outlook which in turn has shaped our political ideology, which has further led to formulation of India's strategic and military thought. The influences of these philosophical strategic cultural forms are far reaching. Table 1 analyses how spiritual thoughts and their corresponding psychological thoughts, political ideology and strategic and military cultures have evolved.

| Spiritual Belief | Psychological Outlook | Political Ideology | Strategic Thought |
|---|---|---|---|
| Spiritual Enlightenment | Reasoning and Thinking | Secularism, Rationalism, Individualism | Sovereignty, Responsibility of Military to protect Sovereignty |
| Salvation and Ethical Life | Centrality of Containment and Humanism | Importance to Civil Rights, Liberalism, Rule of Law, and Democracy | |
| Religious Morality | Centrality of Containment | Safeguard Human Existence and Social Equilibrium | |
| Dharma and Moksha | Moral and Ethical Code, Purpose of Life | Justice | Dharma (Just and Righteous War) as Basis of War fighting |
| Karma | Deservingness, Adaptation, Coping Process, Adjustment | Action, Outcome, Relationship | |
| Equality between truthfulness and God | Moral Responsibility for Upholding Righteousness | Morality and Just Cause | |
| Religious Morality and Salvation | Universal Humanism, Tolerance | Peaceful Co-existence | Non-alignment and Satyagraha (Truth-force) |
| Sewa Dharma (One's Own Duty) Vasudhaiva Kutumbakam (World is one family) | Maintaining Peace, Non-violence | Peaceful Resolution of Conflicts | |

**Table 1**

## Trade, Culture, Interstate Relations: The Frontrunners of Indian Strategic Thought

In between age of the epics and the British Raj, there have been many dynasties that have waxed and waned over centuries or decades, from which a large number of literatures, oral traditions and behaviours have spawned. The current *Pauranic* literatures have been consolidated till as late as the *Gupta* period in the 5th Century CE; similarly the *Sangam* (Classic Tamil literature) literature offers a much broader study of the South Indian strategic culture in their relations with ally and rival states in the period of the three kingdoms of *Cheras*, *Cholas* and *Pandyas*. The *Bakhars* on the Maratha confederacies, the *Rajatarangini* (River of Kings) on the Kashmiri rulers, although liberally brushed in poetry and court flattery, do offer insights into the interstate relations of the time.

Scene from the film "Pardesi" 1958. Soviet actor Oleg Strizhenov as Russian merchant Afanasy Nikitin, who reached India even before Vasco da Gama.

**Image 1**

Most surprising is the sheer lack of attention to the *Mauryas* and the Mughals, both of whose main leaders, Ashoka, and Akbar, are lauded for their tolerance towards their subjects; their interstate relations are completely ignored, when in fact, both of these reigns have

**Image 2**

written records not only in their country but also in other states, where their rule had left an impact. Ashoka's cultural outreach to Sri Lanka, Egypt, Nepal, and a few principalities of China; Akbar's trade outreach to Europe in arms markets, and even the Guptas' trade outreach that linked to Rome but had settled outposts in African kingdoms were all equally important in their interstate relations, as such economic interdependencies are today. The *Cholas* were not part of a small period of expansionist tendencies in the South Asian waters but were a part of series of consecutive outreaches, both cultural and economic, into the neighbouring parts of their kingdoms.

## Strategic Thoughts Post Independence

**1947-1960s**. India's strategic thought process was heavily influenced by its colonial past and the struggle for independence. The immediate priorities were nation-building, economic development and securing territorial integrity. India adopted a policy of non-alignment, refusing to align itself with any major power bloc during the Cold War. This policy aimed at maintaining sovereignty and independence in foreign affairs. The emphasis was on state-led economic development through centralised planning, known as the 'Mixed Economy' model, which included state ownership of key industries and a focus on import substitution industrialisation.

**1960s-1970s**. India faced security challenges, including wars with Pakistan and China. These conflicts reinforced the importance of a strong defence and self-sufficiency in defence production. Despite the non-aligned stance, India developed closer

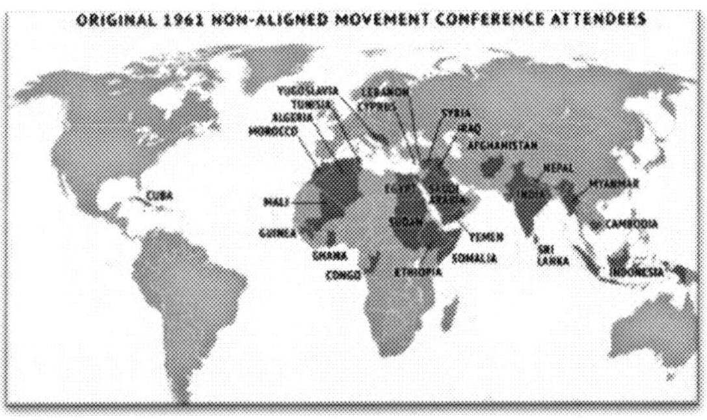


**Image 3**

ties with the Soviet Union, particularly in defence and economic cooperation. The Green Revolution was initiated in the 1960s to boost agricultural productivity and food security, addressing a key strategic concern.

**1970s-1980s**. The 1971 Indo-Pak war resulted in the creation of Bangladesh and further solidified India's strategic posture in the region. India faced economic challenges, including high inflation and balance of payments issues, leading to the initiation of limited economic reforms in the late 1970s and early 1980s.The Soviet invasion of Afghanistan in 1979 and subsequent United States' (US) support for Pakistan had implications for India's strategic calculus, leading to concerns about regional stability and security. By the late 1980s, India's economy was struggling with low growth rates, fiscal deficits, and a balance of payments crisis. The collapse of the Soviet Union and the end of the Cold War necessitated a reassessment of India's foreign policy and strategic priorities. With the diminishing relevance of non-alignment, India sought to adapt to the changing global geopolitical landscape.

**1991**. Economic Liberalisation. The balance of payments crisis in 1991 forced India to undertake significant economic reforms. The reforms, often referred to as the 'New Economic Policy', aimed at liberalising the economy, dismantling many of the protectionist measures, and opening up to foreign investment and trade. This marked a significant shift in India's strategic thought process, as the focus shifted towards integrating with the global economy, attracting foreign investment, and enhancing economic competitiveness. The economic reforms also

THE HINDU

Narasimha Rao's 1991 Budget: the day that changed India forever

Image 4

had implications for India's defence and security strategies, as greater economic strength was seen as essential for maintaining a credible defence posture and addressing security challenges.

**1990s-2000s**. The economic liberalisation initiated in 1991 continued throughout the 1990s and 2000s, leading to significant growth in various sectors of the economy, including Infrormation Technology (IT), telecommunications, and services. India's foreign policy evolved to focus on improving relations with major powers such as the US, while also deepening engagement with countries in East Asia, Africa, and the Middle East. The nuclear tests conducted by India in 1998 marked a significant milestone in India's strategic thought process, underscoring its nuclear capabilities and shaping its nuclear doctrine based on 'Credible Minimum Deterrence'.

**Image 5**

**2010-2023**. India's strategic thought continued to prioritise strategic partnerships with major powers while also increasing its engagement with multilateral institutions. Security challenges persisted, including terrorism, border disputes and regional instability. India faced heightened tensions

**Image 6**

with Pakistan, particularly after terrorist attacks such as the 2008 Mumbai attacks and the 2019 Pulwama attack. The 'Act East Policy', launched in the 2010s aimed at strengthening India's ties with Southeast Asian countries and enhancing its strategic presence in the Indo-Pacific region. The COVID-19 pandemic in 2020 had significant socio-economic implications, leading to disruptions in economic activities, healthcare challenges and the need for rapid policy responses to mitigate the impact. Economic diplomacy became paramount, fostering regional integration and connectivity. Geopolitical tensions, particularly with China, escalated following border clashes in 2020, leading to increased scrutiny of India's strategic posture and defence preparedness. India also prioritised cybersecurity and technological advancements while advocating for climate change mitigation. Throughout, India upheld principles of sovereignty and non-alignment, actively engaging with the global community to safeguard its interests and promote world stability.

## Future Strategic Challenges

**Rising Power Competition**. The intensifying competition between major powers, particularly the US and China, is likely to impact India's strategic calculus. India will need to navigate this competition carefully, balancing its relations with both powers while safeguarding its national interests and sovereignty.

**Regional Instability. Instability**. In India's neighbourhood, including ongoing conflicts, political instability, and terrorism, present significant challenges to India's security. Managing these regional dynamics, fostering stability, and preventing spillover effects will remain key priorities for India's strategic planners.

**Cybersecurity Threats**. With increasing digitisation and reliance on IT, cybersecurity threats are likely to grow in complexity and frequency. India will need to strengthen its cybersecurity capabilities, enhance resilience against cyber-attacks and develop robust cyber defence strategies to mitigate these threats effectively.

**Technological Disruptions**. Rapid advancements in technology, including artificial intelligence, quantum computing and biotechnology, pose both opportunities and challenges for India's security and strategic interests. India will need to invest in research and development, enhance technological innovation and adapt its defence capabilities to keep pace with emerging technologies.

**Climate Change and Environmental Security**. Climate change-induced disasters, resource scarcity and environmental degradation pose significant challenges to India's security and stability. India will need to develop climate resilience strategies, promote sustainable development practices, and cooperate with regional and international partners to address environmental challenges effectively.

## Contours of India's Contemporary Strategic Thought

**Strategic Autonomy**. In the foreseeable future, strategic autonomy is poised to emerge as a central tenet of India's strategic thought, reflecting its commitment to safeguarding national interests and asserting independence in the global arena. With geopolitical dynamics becoming increasingly complex and power competition intensifying, India recognises the importance of maintaining autonomy in its foreign policy decisions and defence posture. India will seek to cultivate diverse partnerships, engage in multi-alignment, and pursue a balanced approach in its international engagements. By asserting strategic autonomy, India aims to uphold its principles of non-alignment, promote peace and stability in the region and advance its national interests on the global stage while retaining the flexibility to adapt to evolving geopolitical realities. This strategic posture underscores India's aspiration to carve out its unique path in the international arena, leveraging its strengths as a rising power to shape the contours of a multipolar world order.

**Economic Diplomacy and Self-Reliance**. In the foreseeable future, India's strategic thought is likely to centre significantly around economic diplomacy and self-reliance as key pillars of its national strategy. Recognising the importance of economic engagement in a rapidly evolving global landscape, India needs to prioritise economic diplomacy to attract foreign investment, foster robust trade relationships and promote its economic interests on the world stage. Embracing the concept of self-reliance, initiatives like Make in India and *Atmanirbhar Bharat* (Self-reliant India) should gain further prominence, aiming to bolster domestic manufacturing capabilities and reduce dependency on imports across critical sectors. This strategic approach will underscore India's aspiration to enhance its economic resilience, mitigate external vulnerabilities and assert its autonomy in shaping its economic destiny.

**Regional Stability and Cooperation**. In the future, India's strategic thought should prioritise regional stability and cooperation aiming to foster peaceful relations and mutual prosperity among neighbouring countries.

**Multilateralism and Global Governance**. Down the line, India's strategic thought should increasingly emphasise multilateralism and global governance as essential pillars of its foreign policy. Recognising the interconnected nature of contemporary challenges, India must advocate for effective multilateral institutions, uphold international norms, and engage in collaborative efforts to address global issues such as climate change, pandemics, and terrorism.

**Leveraging Non-State Actors**. Non-state actors, such as civil society organisations, private companies, and international non-governmental organisations, possess unique capabilities and networks that can complement state efforts in areas like counterterrorism, disaster response and humanitarian aid. Leveraging these actors can enhance India's agility and effectiveness in addressing complex security threats while also fostering goodwill and cooperation on the international stage. Moreover, partnerships with non-state actors can help bridge gaps in governance and capacity, contributing to more resilient and sustainable security solutions.

**Defence Modernisation and Technological Innovation**. In the realm of defence modernisation and technological innovation, India must prioritise substantial investments in research, development, and modernisation efforts to bolster its military capabilities. This includes upgrading equipment, enhancing training, and adopting cutting-edge technologies to effectively address emerging security challenges. Cyber threats and asymmetric warfare, in particular, demand proactive measures such as developing robust cybersecurity frameworks, enhancing intelligence capabilities and investing in advanced defence systems to safeguard national security interests.

**Maritime Security**. Given India's extensive coastline and maritime interests, India must place significant emphasis on maritime security in the Indian Ocean region. The 'Security And Growth for All in the Region' (SAGAR) doctrine underscores India's commitment to ensuring freedom of navigation, combating piracy, and enhancing maritime cooperation with regional partners.

**Counterterrorism and Internal Security**. India remains committed to combating terrorism and extremism, both domestically and internationally. It must focus on intelligence-sharing, border security measures and international cooperation to address cross-border terrorism threats and internal security challenges.

**Soft Power and Cultural Diplomacy**. India can leverage its rich cultural heritage and soft power assets to enhance global influence through cultural diplomacy, by promoting cultural exchange programs, supporting artistic initiatives, and fostering people-to-people ties.

**Image 7**

## Conclusion

Today, as India emerges as a significant player on the global stage, its strategic thought reflects a delicate balance between tradition and innovation, heritage, and modernity. Against the backdrop of evolving geopolitical dynamics, India's strategic thought continues to evolve, drawing upon its rich historical legacy while adapting to the complexities of the modern world.

## End Notes

[1] A History of Religious Ideas: From the Stone Age to the Eleusinian Mysteries Eliade, M. (1978)

[2] Upanishads, Great thinkers of the Eastern World (pp. 155-160), Hundersmarck, L.F. (1995).

[3] Ibid.

[4] On the Vedas, Sri Aurobindo (1956, Pondicherry: Sri Aurobindo International University Centre).

[5] The Classical Law of India, University of California Press, Robert Lingat, 1973.

[6] A Panorama of Indian Culture: Professor A. Sreedhara Menon Felicitation Volume edited by K.K. Kusuman.

3

# *Adnyapatra* and India's Strategic Culture: A Historical Analysis and Contemporary Reflections

**Colonel Amit S Parolekar**

**Abstract**

*This research article delves into the concept of strategic culture, tracing its roots back to the term's inception. The idea has since evolved, and scholars worldwide have explored its relevance in various contexts. In 1992, a United States' researcher, had argued that India lacks strategic culture. This article aims to contribute to the discourse by examining the Adnyapatra (Royal Edict), a 1715 treatise written by Ramchandrapant, shedding light on the era of Chhatrapati Shivaji Maharaj and subsequent rulers of the Maratha Empire. The research explores the translated version of Adnyapatra, providing insights into the 17th Century, drawing parallels with contemporary strategic concepts. In addition to emphasising upon the importance of history and endeavouring to explore the existence of strategic culture, the article eventually raises questions about its impact on a nation's progress and success. It concludes by emphasising the essence of critical analysis to refine and shape India's strategic culture for the challenges of the future.*

## What is Strategic Culture?

The term 'Strategic Culture' was coined by Jack Synder in 1977 in his report prepared for the RAND Corporation, 'The Soviet Strategic Culture: Implications for Limited Nuclear Options'. He emphasised on uniqueness of Soviet strategic thought and its likelihood of responding to a limited nuclear strike by the United States.[1] He said that strategic culture could be defined as the sum total of ideas, conditioned emotional responses and patterns of habitual behaviour, that members of a national strategic community have acquired through instruction or imitation and share with each other with regard to nuclear strategy.[2] Subsequently many think tanks and scholars have picked up the phrase and gone on to put across their perception and understanding of this term. Like civilisations and cultures world over, the term too has matured changing its overtures and graduating to its current understanding which does not find a universal congruence but has a ubiquitous usage. A decade and a half later, in 1992, George Tanham, another RAND researcher expressed his views stating that India lacked a strategic culture to support its emerging geopolitical ambitions.[3] Presumably, the argument has been rebutted by a greater number of Indians, than the number of Americans who have read it. This article endeavours to add to the discourse by examining an Indian historical document *Adnyapatra* (Royal Edict).

The moot question, to begin with is, what is the Indian perspective of strategic culture? In simple terms, it can be defined as the manner in which a nation thinks and conducts itself in addressing the present and the anticipated future, based on its learnings of the past. Therefore, it is an ever-evolving phenomenon. However, most scholars have commented upon the existence of strategic culture in India either through the lens of *Ramayana* and *Mahabharata* or Kautilya's *Arthashastra* (Economics). It is noteworthy to mention that the Indian subcontinent has been the birth place of four major religions and numerous regional leaders and rulers. The essence of the religions, that is, peaceful co-existence and being all accommodative, clubbed with the traditions of myriad rulers and kingdoms have enriched India's strategic culture. Therefore, it would be logical to state that, each empire had its own strategic thought which helped them grow and remain relevant and likewise; each one of them who failed to evolve also diminished into oblivion.

After all, thinkers have also opined that India's strategic culture is not monolithic, rather it is mosaic like, yet distinct, coherent, and contemporary.[4] *Mauryas, Cholas, Pandyas, Gupta, Chalukyas, Ahoms and Marathas* are a few empires amongst many great empires which arose from regional to national powers and shaped the nation's values. These regional perspectives have also added a new dimension to India's strategic culture and hence the merit in studying from the point of view of prevalent strategic thinking of the erstwhile period and its influence on the current era of thinkers. However, as Kanti Bajpai (Indian political scientist) says, "In order to be unbiased, one must guard against the folly of earlier anticipations of later doctrines."[5]

## Analysing the *Adnyapatra* of *Maratha* Empire

Navigating amongst the many great Indian empires, this article focuses on the Maratha empire and endeavours to put forth a perspective of strategic thought prevalent in that era by examining *Adnyapatra, a* treatise written by Ramchandrapant in 1715, based on the governing principles of Chhatrapati Shivaji Maharaj's era. It gives one an insight into 'India's Strategic Culture' of the 17$^{th}$ and 18$^{th}$ Centuries, Ramchandrapant's writing is significant as he was one of the *Ashta Pradhan* (Council of eight ministers) during establishing of *Swarajya* (Self-rule) under Chhatrapati Shivaji. Additionally, he played a crucial role in its protection under Rajaram and Tarabai. Subsequently, his insightful advice based on the principles of Shivaji Maharaj, steered the Maratha empire, during the civil war between Tarabai and Shahu, thereby, witnessing nearly four pioneering generations of the Maratha Empire.[6]

The original document, *Adnyapatra* is known to have been written in the Modi script and transliterated line by line in Marathi language by Prof AR Kulkarni. A copy of *Adnyapatra,* translated in English by Prof SV Puntambekar, available in the open source, as part of the Journal of Indian History. This translation has been utilised to analyse and present arguments in this article.[7]

Research scholars have translated the *Adnyapatra* into nine chapters with the first two chapters highlighting the geopolitical setup and challenges during and post the Shivaji era and hence are rightfully named as 'Troubles of the Kingdom during War of Independence'. The third chapter is named, 'The General Principles of State Policy and Organisation' and it focuses upon the origin of the Kingship culture and lays emphasis on the personal conduct and policy directives for the same. The fourth chapter named, 'Administrative and Ministerial Policy and Organisation' dwells upon the necessity, qualification, and functions of ministers as well as their interpersonal relations and the King's policy towards them. 'Commercial Policy', is the fifth chapter which puts forth policies governing trade and commerce. The sixth chapter named, 'Policy towards *'Watandars'* (Landholders) articulates policies for governing officials involved in the administration. The seventh chapter named, 'Policy Regarding Hereditary '*Vrittis* and *Inams'* (Land Revenue Grants) cautions against nepotism and hereditary transfer of lands even for religious setups. 'Policy about Forts and their Construction and Organisation', is the eighth chapter and as the name suggests speaks about the construction and administration of forts. There is an independent chapter on maritime aspects called, 'Naval Policy' and is the ninth and last chapter of the document.[8] Certain key tenets which emerge post consolidated understanding of the *Adnyapatra* are highlighted in the succeeding paragraphs.

## Key Tenets of *Adnyapatra*

**Rule of Law**. The text highlights the essence of considering the history and then consolidating, demarcating, and building a clear boundary of the kingdom. It supposedly takes cue from Kautilya without his mention as it encapsulates the principles of *Saam* (Persuasion), *Daam* (Rewards to allies and coercion to adversaries), *Dand* (Punishment) *and Bhed* (Division), in order to eliminate anti-social and anti-state inimical elements, both individual as well as fiefdoms. It then goes on to articulate a set of rules and laws which are applicable to all citizens of the kingdom and also dwell on additional restrictions, privileges and guidelines for the ruler himself, emphasising on the reputation of the ruler being synonymous to the character of the kingdom.[9] In the modern-day India, one sees the essence of this understanding in the 'Constitution of India', which assures each citizen of the country with justice, equality, and liberty. In a stark similarity, our history has also witnessed the employment of *Saam, Daam, Dand* and *Bhed* in integrating various princely states into India, post-independence.

**Government and Governance**. *Adnyapatra* highlights myriad functions of the kingdom and considers them broadly under two verticals, administration and military functions. While the king remains at the apex of the entire governing mechanism, there are far too many functions, responsibilities, and diverse areas of governance to be directly addressed by him. Therefore, it puts forth the necessity of appointing meritorious representatives to conduct affairs of the kingdom on his behalf. It also highlights the essence of identification and qualification of the appointed representatives and emphasises of their prudence and functioning along with their inter-representative and king-representative working relations.[10] Looking at the democratic setup of India, through the lens of this document, one sees the elected leader as the ruler, the civil servants under distinct ministries and the armed forces as the instruments for effective governance. The qualification, selection and functioning of the bureaucrats and the armed force personnel are well established and are in consonance with the administrative and the ministerial policy of the *Adnyapatra*. To incorporate the values of democracy into this setup, one has the elected representatives functioning as various ministers to ensure a vibrant democracy. There also lies the important responsibility and power of the common citizen to elect befitting candidates as their representatives. Evidently, the current system, like the Maratha State, is all inclusive and flexible as is essential for effective functioning of the nation state. The concept of *Ashta Pradhan*, which comprised of *Pant Pradhan* (Prime Minister); *Pant Amatya* (Finance and Auditor General of Accounts); *Pant Sachiv* or *Soornees* (Secretary of Documentation); *Mantri* or *Waknis* (Minister of Internal and private affairs); *Sarnaubat* or *Senapati* (Commander of the Armed Forces); *Pant Sumant* or *Dubeer* (Minister of External Affairs including trade); *Nyayadheesh* (Judiciary Minister) and *Panditrao Danadhyaksha* (Miniter of Religious Affairs). These appointments were not hereditary, but were based on meritocracy, which is in sync with the democratic setup of council of ministers.[11]

**Trade and Commerce**. Trade is the prime source of prosperity for any kingdom. The merchants must hence be respected, but the trade must be governed very strictly, and policies must favour the growth and well-being of the kingdom, not the traders. It lays out the essence of making one's kingdom an attractive and preferred location for settling and proliferation of trade. On the other hand, it also cautions against certain merchants who secretively nurture political and expansionist ambitions and articulates strict guidelines for dealing with them.[12] The importance of import and export directly affects a country's Gross Domestic Product, exchange rates and inflation.[13] The growing impetus on *Atmanirbharta* (Self-reliance) and the ease of doing business in India are governing principles which have the texture of the commercial policy of the Maratha State.

**Federal Governance**. The Maratha kingdom had numerous *Watandars* who initially had hereditary rights and functioned as independent chiefs of small portions of territories. Invariably, each one aspired to expand and improve his territory. Occasionally, they also either connived or took refuge from certain invading armies against the state. On this pretext some *watandars* aspired to keep a separate military for defence purpose which was denied as a state policy. Nonetheless, their security, and appropriate degree of freedom in functioning needed a charter. This was clearly articulated in the 'Policy towards *Watanadars*', which established the mechanism of the King's policy towards them.[14] The federal structure of the country's governing setup, clear distinction of central and state subjects, strict centrality of defence forces and centre-state relations are concepts which appear as mirror image of the erstwhile Maratha State.

**Essence of Potent Armed Forces**. The last two chapters of *Adnyapatra*, elucidate in great detail about the essence of forts, their construction and governance mechanism followed by the construction, organisation, and importance of maritime capability. It emphasises that protecting oneself is more important than annihilating the enemy.[15] The forts, which were the mainstay of defence, warfighting and military governance of the erstwhile era can be seen as synonymous with the current day armed forces. Drawing a parallel from the historical text, the selection, training, grooming, and upgrading of the armed forces is the primary depiction of self-defence capability. They may not be employed for cross border action, but their existence and the currency of their capability is the most vital defence mechanism of the nation state. Similarly, the navy is an independent arm of state functioning.[16] It is not merely meant for fighting the naval battles but is essential for ensuring maritime dominance. The *Adnyapatra* talks about different types of ships, their utility, and the overall organisation into a comprehensive instrument of state policy.[17] This aspect finds reality in the variety of class and category of ships being held with Indian Navy. The methodology of naval warfighting as mentioned in *Adnyapatra* may vary largely with our current maritime concept of operations, but seemingly is similar in spirit to achieve victory.

## Does India have a Strategic Culture?

The analysis of the *Adnyapatra* and the understanding of the derivative key tenets not only highlight the existence of rich strategic culture in the 17$^{th}$ Century era, but also indicates the influence of the regional thought and dimensions in the current strategic framework. It is also indicative of how the thinking has proliferated through centuries from the Vedic ages to different empires which have flourished on the Indian soil. Each subsequent empire has incorporated and suitably modified the tenets of administration and warfare to the contemporary requirements, thereby, further enriching the strategic culture. The research article can draw a partial conclusion at this juncture, as the rich statecraft document of Shivaji's era, *Adnyapatra*, has been examined and its parallels in contemporary times have been cited. These findings are indicative of the existence of a rich strategic culture in the 17$^{th}$ and 18$^{th}$ centuries as well as in present times.

## An Alternate Thought

Alternatively, a counter argument is: that If the Maratha empire had such a rich strategic culture, why did it not flourish beyond two centuries? As a thinking military mind, certain other questions which must also intrigue are, as to what is the big concern about existence or absence of strategic culture? Does the proof of its existence guarantee assured success in all conflicts across all eras? Does the lack of strategic culture indicate an existential threat to the nation? While there may not be instant answers to these questions, considering strategic culture as a nation's decision-making and policy-formulating ability based on its experience and prevailing value system could offer a new line of thinking. Amongst the four variables cited above, the latter two evolve with time. However, the first two, namely decision-making and policy-formulating abilities, are tenets for which leaders at all levels and in all domains must train and educate themselves. It would not only enrich the nation's strategic culture but would also guide it on the path of progress.

Another dimension of strategic culture which merits to be commented upon is its shapers and carriers. The shapers of strategic culture of any nation are primarily political party leaders, notably politicians and ministers, senior bureaucratic officials, print and electronic media, think tanks, senior military officers, universities, and academicians.[18] On the other hand, the carriers or so to say the reflectors of strategic culture are the political hierarchy at large.[19] Therefore, when certain research scholars argue about the absence of strategic thought or culture, it would be prudent to analyse the leadership and political dispensation of the period. It would only be fair to assume that the reflectors of the strategic culture may not have been vibrant enough for others to register, but by no means it is indicative of the absence of strategic culture in that nation state. Therefore, as professional military leaders, it is imperative to engross into marathons of analytical readings and critical writings, which add different dimensions in understanding, shaping and refining India's strategic culture. Afterall, only a well-shaped culture, can be reflected well.

## Conclusion

*Adnyapatra*, authored by Ramchandrapant in 1715, offers a unique window into the strategic culture of the Maratha era, governed by the principles of Chhatrapati Shivaji Maharaj. Analysing the document, brings forth the strategic acumen that propelled the Marathas from a regional power to a national empire, contributing to the shaping of strategic thought of subsequent eras. In essence, the analysis of *Adnyapatra* not only sheds light on the strategic culture of the 17$^{th}$ and 18$^{th}$ Centuries but also invites one to engage in a continuous dialogue with the historical roots, fostering a more comprehensive understanding of India's strategic thought and its enduring relevance. In embracing the complexity and dynamism of India's strategic culture, one must acknowledge that the lessons from the Maratha era continue to resonate in the present geopolitical landscape. At the same time, questioning the status quo and critical analysis of historical as well as contemporary governing principles and thoughts will pave the way for a more informed and a nuanced approach to navigating the challenges of the future, thereby, further evolving the strategic culture.

## End Notes

[1] Jack L Synder, The Soviet Strategic Culture: Implications for Limited Nuclear Operations, RAND Corporation Report R-2154-AF, Sep 1977, page v, accessed as an open-source document on 01 Feb 2024.

[2] Ibid. page 8.

[3] AVM Arjun Subramaiam, Does India have a strategic culture? Newspaper article published in Times of India; 04 Feb 2016 accessed as an open-source document on 01 Feb 2024.

[4] Rodney W Jones, India's Strategic Culture, Report prepared for US Defense Threat Reduction Agency on 31 Oct 2006, page 3, accessed on open source on 01 Feb 2024.

[5] Kanti Bajpai, 'State, Society, Strategy', in Kanti Bajpai and Amitabh Matoo (editors), Securing India: Strategic Thought and Practice, Manohar Publications, Page 83-84.

[6] S V Puntambekar, erstwhile political scientist and professor at Benaras Hindu University, in his English translation of the Marathi transliteration of Adnyapatra by Prof A R Kulkarni, Introduction, *Journal of Indian History*, n.d, Page 11/81. This being the mother document, has been cited on multiple occasions and has been simply written as "Adnyapatra" herein after.

[7] Ramchandra Pant Amatya, Adnyapatra, https://archive.org/details/Adnyapatra/mode/2up, dated 02 Sep 2021

[8] Ibid, Adnyapatra, page 11

[9] Ibid, Adnyapatra, page 83-104

[10] Ibid, Adnyapatra, page 207-211

[11] https://www.youtube.com/watch?v=m553OMIvww4, YouTube video, "Ashta Pradhan Mandal of Shivray" in Marathi by Omkar Gujar, accessed on 02 Feb 2024.

[12] Adnyapatra, page 212-213

[13] Leslie Kramer, "How Importing and Exporting Impacts the Economy", https://www.investopedia.com/articles/investing/100813/interesting-facts-about-imports-and- exports.asp#toc-economic-reports 27 Sep 2023

[14] op cit, Adnyapatra, page 214-215

[15] op cit, Adnyapatra, page 219-232

[16] op cit, Adnyapatra, page 229

[17] op cit, Adnyapatra, page 229-230

[18] Rodney W Jones, India's Strategic Culture, Report prepared for US Defense Threat Reduction Agency on 31 Oct 2006, page 28, accessed on open source on 01 Feb 2024

[19] Ibid.

# 4

# Thirukural: Demystifying an Ancient Text and Seeking its Significance in Contemporary Statecraft

**Brigadier D Seshasai Murty, SC, SM****

**Abstract**

*Thiruvalluvur in writing the Thirukkural (Sacred Verses) has exposed the depth of wisdom that existed nearly 2000 years ago. It makes knowing and deciphering the Kurals a task of discovery, awareness and awakening. The literature available on Thiruvalluvur is very limited and calls for greater focus. The timelessness of what each Kural states, its application individually and for the society as a whole for eternity, must never be lost. In learning from our ancient texts, it would be prudent to have a whole-of-nation approach. The perils of dynastic rules and the impact of invaders have laid to waste so much of India's rich heritage; the rediscovery must be deliberate with an intent to revive what India once was.*

*When envy, rage, lust and foul speech, these four*
*Don't deflect you, you are on virtue's path secure*

*Chapter 4, Verse 35*

## Introduction

A country and civilisation as ancient as India's have innumerable sages and saints, a multitude of literary gems, philosophical thinkers propounding detailed articulations of the ways of life apart from the origins of a few major religions of the world. As followers of the art and science of warfare, there always exists an academic urge to seek guidance from these abundant resources, the most famous being the *Arthashastra* (Economics) by Chanakya. On the other hand, the '*Thirukkural*' (Sacred Verses) by Tiruvalluvar has been a more recent discovery and perhaps a welcome addition to India's rich heritage.

*Thirukkural* as a book, deals with the art of living and transcends national boundaries, social limitations and language barriers.[1] It has been divided into three parts on the worldly human aspects of 'Virtue', 'Wealth' and 'Love'. The three parts consist of 133 chapters containing a total of 1330 'Kurals'. The uninitiated needs to understand that *Thiru* means sacred, beautiful etc., and *Kural* is the measure which means anything short. An exposure to the *Kurals* shows how each couplet conveys maximum sense in minimum words.[2] It is appealing to the mind, sweet to the ear and delicious to the tongue.

*Those with pure mind and studied eloquence*
*Should use words that suit the audience*

*Chapter 72, Verse 711*

The *Thirukkural* is traditionally dated to the immediate Post-*Sangam* Period (Early Medieval Period), referring to the era of the Tamil *Sangams (*Academies) that are said to have flourished between 300 BCE and 300 CE.[3] The existence of the author and a single author having written and compiled the *Thirukkural* is a matter of historical study and establishment. However, the essence of the compositions and the continuity of thought and expression are but evidence of a timeless work by a learned and sagacious person. The mere fact that the *Kurals* have found meaning in the lives of the greats who have lived amongst them due to their timeless principles on governance, ethics, and leadership, justifies their greatness. The *Thirukkural* remains the most translated and cited work of Tamil literature.[4]

*No one's 'born noble' on this earth*
*Conduct makes you trustworthy, not birth*

*Chapter 14, Verse 133*

## A Historical Perspective

Historically, the *Thirukkural* and Thiruvalluvur have not been associated with any reign or kingdom. There exists no mention in the enunciation of the *Kurals* of such association or linkage. This makes it difficult to relate the work to a definite period. *Valluvar's* Tamil country exhibits disparities, encompassing both affluent individuals and those in destitution. It experiences both splendour and squalor, as well as literacy and ignorance.[5] It knows disease and system of medicine. It has a place for the arts; forbear of modern *Sabhas* (Meetings), and as it has courts, so does it have courtesans.[6] The abundance of wisdom depicted in the *Thirukkural*, as is evident and has been stated by various researchers defines an era of rules and discipline; an era of peace and prosperity. This could have been anywhere in South India where empires and dynasties flourished from 7th Century BCE and up to the 13th Century CE.

Tamil dynasties are the kingdoms that ruled over present day Tamil Nadu, Sri Lanka, Andhra Pradesh, Karnataka, Kerala and Odisha. These include the *Pallavas*, the *Pandyas*, the *Cholas* and the *Cheras.*[7] A look into these reveals the vast extent of their reach extending even beyond peninsular India, to include South East Asia. However, the scriptures, constructions and remnants of those times, which are abundant, do not reveal any kind of linkage of the *Thirukkural* or the venerable author Thiruvalluvar with any of them.

The first translation of the *Kurals* is believed to be of 1595 CE in Malayalam but went unnoticed. It was again discovered by the Christian missionaries and translated into English, Latin and French in the 16th and 17th Centuries. The *Kural* text has enjoyed a universal appeal right from antiquity owing to its secular and non-denominational nature, which suited the sensibilities of all. The universality is such that, despite its having been written in the pre-Christian era, almost every religious group in India and across the world, including Christianity, has claimed the work for itself.[8] On date, it has been translated into 42 world languages, with more than 50 renditions in English itself; the largest for a non-religious work of ancient literature.

What one wants to learn is also dictated by what one wants to practice. The enabling factor in this loop of learn and practice is the profession; every profession as it exists today can learn and practice what has been conveyed in the *Thirukkural*. As an example of its application, a verse as applied to human resource management is reproduced.

*No one is perfectly learned, no one perfectly wise*
*A lack here, a fault there need come as no surprise*

*Chapter 51, Verse 503*

### A Glimpse of Statecraft

Statecraft can be defined as the skilled management of state affairs. *Kautilya's Arthashastra* is widely regarded as the most comprehensive compilation from ancient texts on this subject., giving out in detail, of how a state has to be governed. Statecraft in ancient India subsumes international relations. The primary end goal and the 'Conceptual Hook' in Kautilya's *Arthashastra* is *yogakshema*, where '*Yoga*' means action or acquisition of things, and '*Kshema*' is consolidation or secure possession. Together, this umbrella concept ensures '*Raksha*' (Security) and '*Palana*' (Well-being) of the people. This dual task is performed through a political economic approach which meaningfully interweaves '*Dandaniti*' (Political science) and *vartta* (Economics); the domestic '*Tantra*' (Realm) and the '*Avapa*' (Interstate) material well-being of the people uphold political legitimacy and sustain social cohesion, resulting in gainful economic production. This, in turn, strengthens the '*Danda*' (Rod) wielded by the king in the international realm, and advances security of the kingdom.

In modern times, statecraft has evolved to encompass the entire spectrum of governance, regardless of its form. The ancient texts dwell upon the primacy of the king or the ruler which translates to the government in power today. So, what are the aspects of statecraft that can be thought of as they exist today? This to any mind, will encompass how the country conducts itself diplomatically, economically and militarily in the world forum to express and abide by its national interests. In reference to India, the people as a nation have exhibited peaceful and non-aligned core values as an expression of the foundational ethics and values that are cherished and how these are manifested in the character and dealings, both internally and externally. This can be taken as a benchmark to discuss the timeless compositions of Thiruvulluvur to try and seek its significance for contemporary statecraft.

*People regard the King as God*
*For just rule and guard*

*Chapter 39, Verse 388*

A country that has 'Just Rule' will find favour in the comity of nations. Just rule will imply good democratic values and equitable social fabric; it will also indicate the position adopted by the country on various issues of importance such as climate control, upholding of human rights, positions on trade agreements, adoption of international norms etc. Concurrently, as stated in Verse 388, the country that is able to guard itself from internal and external threats will also find a place of favour. This will be from its own people and also from other nations. It will enable close and favourable relations, good diplomatic ties and enduring friendships. Applied in context, nations, that display autocratic and authoritative dispositions (viz. North Korea) find themselves isolated.

## *Thiruvalluvur* and Statecraft

*Thirukkural* by *Thiruvalluvur*, as is known by all is divided into three books; the first consisting of 38 chapters deals with virtues, the second having of 70 chapters is about the various aspects of statecraft and the third with 25 chapters is about love. Chapter 39, the first on statecraft speaks about the qualities of a king which in today's parlance would mean the head of the government or all those in a position of leadership. These qualities enunciated more than 2000 years back hold relevance in present times as well.

*And these four–gutsy, giving, sage and spright*
*A king must be for his kingship to come right*

*Chapter 39, Verse 383*

*Help, grace, poise, devotion*
*Are a mighty king's definition*

*Chapter 39, Verse 390*

Knowledge on professional matters holds prime importance in the execution of statecraft. A diplomat has to have in-depth knowledge of all nations to be able to advise and formulate the terms of engagement with each. Similarly, the economist must be learned and be able to advise and lead the nation's efforts to be strong and competitive. The lack of knowledge and learning when compared to the competing nations will always relegate them to second place.

*The scholar begs for knowledge, the beggar for food*
*To the first we give the stage, to the second a coin crude*

*Chapter 40, Verse 395*

The power of learning and possession of knowledge base is such that it helps to define an individual or a nation. The opportunities provided in a nation enables it to attract such individuals, which adds to the national wealth. In the past, inability to develop the required opportunities because of economic poverty has had an impact in terms of 'Brain Drain', which is now being overcome with vigoured focus. Further, the regions within a nation, which are more literate enjoy a higher standard of living; similarly, nations which were at the fore in the last two centuries stand developed and enjoy a greater say in the power politics of the world. This understanding and the need to address this issue will enable the nation to realise its true potential, with a share of influence in the polity of nations.

*The scholar each land befriends, each town makes its own*
*The unschooled dies at home a nomad, lonesome and unknown*

*Chapter 40, Verse 397*

The world today is enmeshed by the speed of communications, the prevalence of technologies, and the proliferation of conglomerates, leading to the blurring of distances and boundaries. The era of binary relations in statecraft are hardly existing, making diplomacy a hard beast to control. However, what holds true through the ages is the seminal significance of friends and friendships. Nurtured on common ideologies, supported by like-minded thought processes and with agreements on contemporary issues, friends among nations aids diplomacy. It enables direction of stated national interests and the achievement of objectives and goals. Conversely, foes add to woes as stated in the Thirukkural.

*Ten times worse, than incurring the wrath of foes*
*Is to leave friends and face life's woes*

*Chapter 44, Verse 450*

The power of diplomacy in global relations exhibits the power of a nation. The '*Ashwamedha Yajna*' (Horse Sacrifice) of Vedic origin was a tool for exercising diplomatic power over the territories backed by the military might; however, in today's world order it works differently. The recent release of eight ex-Indian Navy personnel by Qatar is a defining example of the power of diplomacy backed by a strong nation and a strong leader. It brings to fore the importance of being able to gauge own strengths and shortcomings in the prosecution of statecraft. As Thiruvalluvur says:

*Weigh the act, your own might, foes might*
*And allies might and proceed straight*

*Chapter 48, Verse 471*

Strength in itself is not an assurance of success. The place and time of the action are as important, if not more. The need to build strength, diplomatically, militarily and economically, enables the creation of comprehensive national power. The application of this comprehensive national power at a suitable time and place enables attainment of stated national objectives. This fundamental of statecraft has been encapsulated by the great Thiruvalluvur in the verses of chapter 49.

*A crow can conquer even an owl in daylight*
*A king needs apt time to put foes to flight*

*Chapter 49, Verse 481*

*Just like a stork, bide your time*
*Act with might, at the right time*

*Chapter 49, Verse 490*

Economy is an irrefutable pillar of a nation's statecraft. The achievement of national objectives and the protection of national interests stems from the might or lack of a strong economy. The world today, to include India, has embarked on the realisation that economic strength and stability are the bedrock of a strong nation. It enables the aspirations of the citizens to be met leading to internal harmony; at the same time, it provides for the nation, a superior platform to deal with other nations on the world forum. This has been so wisely articulated by Thiruvalluvur when he says.

*No weapon of war nears the lethal weapon called wealth*
*Let your foe feel your money's steel and its razor's tensile strength*

*Chapter 76, Verse 759*

Since times immemorial, the might of the army has been touted to be the strength of the ruler. This also holds today, with numerous live examples where the nations' armed forces, a pillar of a nation's statecraft are being wielded to achieve stated aims and interests; the Russia-Ukraine war and the Hamas-Israel conflict are two such examples. The two world wars and their outcomes tell a similar story. The era of the 'Cold War' and how it spawned the arms race and the arms industry is embedded in world history. Nations that boast of large armed forces, suitably organised and modern, are higher up in the pecking order. In the neighbourhood, adversarial nations across borders necessitates round the clock vigil and preparedness. It dictates to have a strong standing force to protect India's interests. How an army should be has been stated by Thiruvalluvar as under:

*An army will surely triumph when it is free*
*From desertion, aversion and penury*

*Chapter 76, Verse 769*

*When tough is the foe, rough the task, terrain and timing snarled*
*Depend on veteran soldiers, of knee and knuckle gnarled*

*Chapter 77, Verse 762*

The wisdom of Thiruvalluvur covers the entire spectrum of what statecraft encompasses. A nation has friends and foes and they need to be engaged with, round the clock, by all instruments at their disposal. To engage with an enemy who is known to be more powerful is dangerous and detrimental, a lesson learned throughout the ages. At the same time, the weak enemy must be thus engaged, crushed and controlled to ensure own development and prosperity.

*Avoid conflict with enemies more powerful*
*Cherish enmity with the less powerful*

*Chapter 87, Verse 861*

In deciding between a friend and a foe, the ethos and culture of a nation have a major influence. Centuries of wisdom makes India a peace loving and benign country, as compared to so many, to include the neighbours. Time and again one has been foolish in believing peace overtures and parleys, to end up with yet another lesson on betrayal. Thiruvalluvur states that those who act with treason must be sought out as enemies and no less.

*Gain at any cost the enmity of one*
*Who acts friendly with treason*

*Chapter 87, Verse 867*

The essence of the execution of statecraft also lies in the selection and employment of the right person in any of the domains. Even in the selection process, the importance of testing, that is, having performed such tasks, has been underscored by Thiruvalluvur.

*Never choose men without judging*
*Assign apt work after choosing*

*Chapter 51, Verse 509*

Information is the second pillar of the diplomatic, informational, military and economic aspects. The importance of information has enhanced vastly over the ages and needs no separate emphasis. The need to have information and the instruments to garner internal and external information was limited to the spies in the ancient times. Chapter 59 encapsulates Thiruvalluvur's wisdom on spies and detectives, on how they should be and how they should work for the King. The need to know what is happening in the kingdom on a daily basis is contained in Verse 582; it reveals the importance of the people and what views they have. This information as described was to enable the king to rule effectively. In today's world there are a host of instruments which act as the barometer on different fields and aid governance.

*What goes on in his realm, who does what and why*
*These the King must learn each day from some reliable spy.*

*Chapter 59, Verse 582*

## Conclusion

The Kurals, all 1330 of them, are a treasure trove and hold meaning for each reader, regardless of their profession or education. It remains for the interested to read, comprehend and then corelate the gospel truths to the existing world. These *Kurals* encompass the real-world situations and dilemmas as they exist today and provide guidance. They transcend the fields occupied by management gurus at one end to the love gurus at the other end. However, the renditions on statecraft have no parallel and each exposure leads to the discovery of the depth and wisdom contained.

There are words for the leadership and the led; there are enunciations for the diplomat and the soldier. The virtues, which define India as an ancient society are provided for in abundance, illuminating a path to be followed. Each iteration leads to a fresh understanding and relevance of the composition; a remarkable attribute of this timeless work. Each translation by numerous researchers has been done differently with the key idea to retain the essence. In reading the different translations, one will pick up how every exposure actually defines a new lesson of life and how it stands to be applied.

## End Notes

[1] Dr M Rajaram, Thirukural : Pearls of Inspiration, Rupa Publications, 01 Apr 2009

[2] Ibid

[3] Gopalkrishna Gandhi, Tiruvalluvar The Tirukkural, Aleph Book Company, 01 Aug 2015

[4] Zvelebil Kanil, The Smile of Murugan : On Tamil Literature of South India, Leiden EJ Brill, Mahajan, ISBN 9004035915

[5] Gopalkrishna Gandhi, Tiruvalluvar The Tirukkural, Aleph Book Company, 01 Aug 2015

[6] Ibid

[7] Jesudasan, Dennis S, Keezhadi Excavations, The Hindu

[8] Zvelebil Kanil, The Smile of Murugan: On Tamil Literature of South India, Leiden EJ Brill, Mahajan, ISBN 9004035915

# 5

# Demystifying the Ahom Dynasty and their Strategic Culture

**Colonel Jyotisman Hazarika**

**Abstract**

*The Ahom dynasty's reign in Northeast India stands as a testament to their military prowess, administrative innovation, and cultural inclusivity. Originating from the Tai-Ahom people who migrated to Northeast India in the 13th Century, they ruled for over six centuries, fostering unity among diverse ethnic tribal groups and celebrating cultural amalgamation. The Ahoms excelled on the battlefield, notably in the campaigns against the Islamic Invaders and the Mughals, and contributed significantly to art, literature, and societal norms. Their strategic culture integrated military and civilian life through the unique Paik (Peasant-soldiers) system, ensuring a balanced army and societal stability. Their decentralised administration, defensive tactics, and emphasis on national security, characterised their rule. This article highlights the Ahom dynasty's remarkable legacy and its relevance in understanding India's rich historical tapestry and strategic culture.*

## Introduction

Unknown to many, there is a remarkable chapter in the history of Northeast India, the reign of the Ahoms. The Ahom dynasty's ascendency in this region is not only a testament to their strength and ingenuity but also a narrative that shapes our understanding of the rich military heritage that our nation possesses.

The Ahom dynasty, originating from the Tai-Ahom people who migrated to the Brahmaputra valley from present day Yunan Region in the 13th Century, established a legacy that spanned more than six centuries. Their reign, marked by astute leadership, unique administration style, cultural vibrancy, and military prowess, has left a permanent mark on the cultural tapestry of Northeast India, especially in the plains of Brahmaputra.

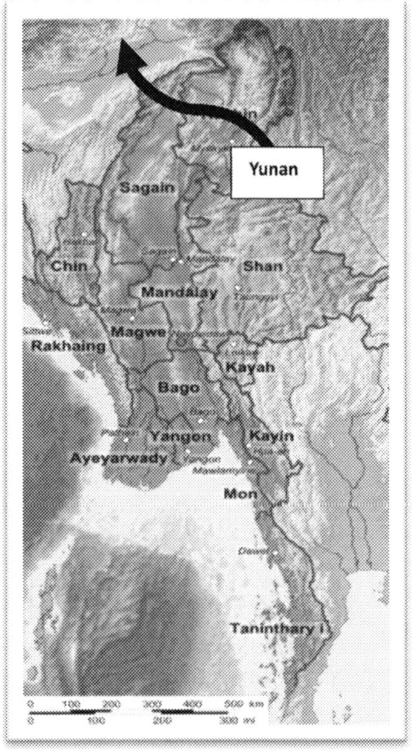


**Map 1**

One of the most striking features of the Ahom dynasty was their ability to foster an environment of harmony and unity amidst the diverse ethnic groups of the region. They created an inclusive society, where cultural amalgamation was celebrated, languages were preserved, and traditions were cherished. Their governance was marked by fairness and a deep understanding of the needs of the people they ruled.

However, it is on the battlefield that the Ahoms truly excelled. Their military strategies and prowess enabled them to resist numerous invasions, ensuring the sovereignty of their land. The famous Battle of Saraighat in 1671, where the Ahom General Lachit Borphukan thwarted the mighty Mughal-Rajput forces under the Rajput King Ram Singh, remains an iconic example of their valour and grit.

The Ahoms' contribution to art, architecture, and literature is also noteworthy. They constructed impressive monuments like the *Rang Ghar* (Amusement House) and *Talatal Ghar* (House of Entertainment), which stand as symbols of their architectural brilliance. Their love for literature led to the creation of literary works like the *Buranjis*, (Historical Chronicles) that provide valuable insights into their rule. This was also the time when Scholar-Saint Shankardev spread Neo-*Vaishnavite* ideals which were very popular and accepted by all sections of the society.

As one reflects upon the Ahom domination in Northeast India, one is reminded of the importance of preserving history and heritage. Their legacy serves as an inspiration for unity, resilience, and cultural richness. It teaches that greatness can be achieved through leadership, inclusivity, and a deep connection to one's roots. The strategic culture prevalent in ancient or medieval India is generally associated with the campaigns of Chandragupta Maurya, expansion of Chola Kingdom in the maritime domain, texts on statecraft like *Arthashastra* (Economics) and Tirrukural (Sacred Verses), or expansionist campaigns of Zorawar Singh and Shivaji. The campaigns of the Ahoms and the way the northeast region of India maintained its sovereignty has hardly been associated with strategic culture of India. Notwithstanding, there has been a recent attempt to acknowledge the contribution of the Ahoms in this context and rightfully place the dynasty in Indian history.

## Distinctive Ahoms: Unveiling the Life and Times of an Unconventional Dynasty

The Ahoms ruled Assam for nearly 600 years, during which they introduced new concepts and elements into the society. These elements brought in a fundamental change in the society driving it towards nationalism which was unseen and unheard of earlier. The history of that period is well-chronicled in the *Buranjis*, travelogues of Muslim travellers from Northern India (*Hindustaan*, as mentioned during that period) and war diaries of 'Mughal Campaigners', mostly in Persian and also the *Charitas* (Charity) of saints of that time.

Prior to the Ahoms, the Assamese society was fragmented with caste-based divisions with major influence of the priests. Even the professions of commoners were significantly influenced by the caste system. Sanskrit was the official language (introduced by *Varman* Dynasty of Bengal), and decisions were taken by the upper sections of the society, though the administration was weak with no proper ruler/kingdom/dynasty. The Ahoms changed it all, once they arrived on the scene. Their integration of the military into the society brought in a strategic culture, wherein, the basic idea of every household contributing to nation-building was the driving force.[1] This thought process is being covered in detail in the next segment.

- **Inclusiveness and Unification**. The Ahom Dynasty ushered in a society with the common man's language, i.e., Assamese, as the state language, and more focus on inclusiveness through professionalism rather than religion. Both Sanskrit and Assamese were used for official purposes and the period saw the growth of Neo-*Vaishnavism* under Srimanta Shankar Dev, a scholar-saint still revered in Assam. The Assamese literature was enriched by many secular writings, and this period also saw the growth in non-religious literature. Some of the great works not known to many in India today includes *Bakul Kayasthas' Kitabat Manjuri* (Mathematical Treatises) and Sridhar's *Sandhyakanda* (An astrological work). The *Buranjis* were another significant contribution by the Ahom rulers to Assamese literature, which were the historical chronicles documenting various episodes or events of history. This period also saw the growth of sports and culture with focus on festivals associated with the seasons, agriculture and to an extent, religion. These initiatives brought the diverse tribal population under a common framework of rules and regulations, which led to a unified Assam. In addition, the Ahom rulers fostered friendship through reconciliatory and efficient diplomatic mechanism with all the local tribal chieftains in the neighbouring hilly regions (including chiefs with tribal followers of less than a few hundreds) beyond the Brahmaputra valley, leading to tribal bonhomie and peaceful coexistence. This ethos ensured a congregation of states which had common goals and foreign policies. This conglomeration remained united and ensured sovereignty of the region despite the aggressionist forces both to its east i.e., Burmese Kingdom and west i.e., Mughals.

❑ **Ahom Dynasty: A Contemporary Comparison with Mughals**. The Ahoms were distinctly different from other dynasties that had moved to the sub-continent from other parts of Asia. It is but obvious to compare the Mughals with the Ahoms, since both communities had moved into the sub-continent from their native states during the same era. However, they were very different in their approach to administration, culture, religion, and other aspects such as politics. The Ahoms did bring in their 'Tai Culture' to the plains of Brahmaputra, but they never forced any of it on the local population. In fact, they seamlessly integrated with the locals and adopted the Assamese culture including their religion, which was and is Hinduism. They did bring in their customs and traditions and infused them into the local customs. Even today, the Ahom community has its culture intact. For example, the community still celebrates their traditional festival called *Me-Dam-Me-Phi* (Offerings made to the departed ancestors and spirits), which is celebrated on 31$^{st}$ Jan every year to worship their ancestors. The Ahom rulers encouraged local festivals like *Magh Bihu* (Harvest Festival) and *Rongali Bihu* (Marks the beginning of the Assamese New Year) and gave them the much-required patronage, which finally led to a state-level celebration accepted by all, across different ethnic groups, tribes and communities; a new symbol of Assamese identity.[2] Interestingly, the coronation ceremony of the Ahom kings was solemnised by both Ahom and Hindu rituals. Practically, all the Ahom kings on ascending to the throne assumed two names, one in Assamese Hindu form and the other in Tai. This makes this dynasty distinctly different from the rest of the invaders, who reached the plains of North India from Central Asian Region in the same period, but could never accept the local culture, religion and the way of life.

❑ **Status of Women in the Society**.[3] During the Ahom rule, the status of women was indeed remarkable for its relatively elevated position, compared to many other contemporary societies across the sub-continent. The high position of women in the Ahom dynasty of Assam can be attributed to a blend of cultural, social, and historical factors that valued their contributions and recognised their civil rights as individuals within the broader framework of the society.

❑ **Economic and Revenue Model**. The economy of the Ahoms was not robust due to the geographic location as the entire region was thickly forested and had limited roads and navigable river network. Agriculture was the backbone of the Ahom's economy. The agrarian economy was self-sufficient, and the people never faced food insecurity. In fact, the plains of Brahmaputra produced adequate crops and provided the hilly tribes with grains, in return for animal and forest products.[4] This barter system added to the bonhomie that was prevalent during that period. Notwithstanding the dominance of agriculture, the wealthy segment of the population still engaged in trade (both internal and external). Despite that, the urban economy failed to develop beyond a certain point due to lack of trade routes and access to the sea. The Ahom period villages were organised in such a way that families with similar professions and ethnic backgrounds were grouped together. Many villages were populated primarily by members of a specific professional community, as evidenced by the names of the villages, such as *Tantikuchi* (Weaving) and *Kamarkuchi* (Pottery). This economic model known as 'Clustering' was encouraged and widely prevalent during that period. The common people were not taxed by the Ahoms. The common man had the option of paying taxes to the king in the form of manual labour as well as fighting in wars as soldiers. This was a unique provision and accordingly the entire community was organised into a militarised hierarchy with emphasis on skill building and military training. The pressure on the citizens was to perform for the growth of the state rather than the heavy taxes, which was the norm across the sub-continent. Since there was no elaborate tax collection, the rulers lived a humble life devoid of grand palaces, forts, royal celebrations, and expensive lifestyle. The entire revenue and efforts were dedicated towards public infrastructure like road-bridges, anti-flood bunds, defence-oriented bunds, store houses, temples etc. Shehabuddin Talesh, an account keeper of the Mughal Army who accompanied Mir Jumla, a Mughal Governor under Aurangazeb writes, "This country, if governed on the pattern of the Mughal administration would fetch revenue of 45,00,000 of rupees annually, including the tax collected from the public and income from the elephants caught from the forest. But collection of taxes from public is not among the customs of this country". (Translated from Persian by Dr Mazhar Asif, Guwahati University).[5]

❑ **Militarised Society**. In addition to these shortcomings of economy, Ahoms had two difficult neighbours to handle the Burmese empire to the east and the Mughals in the west. To balance the territorial security requirement (sovereignty) and the lack of resources, the Ahoms came up with a new form of integrating the societal norms with the military. The system was called the *Paik* (Peasant Soldiers) System and similar to the conscription or reservist system of modern militaries. They also brought in a military hierarchy, infused into the society and specialists were created. The Ahoms created a society which can be loosely called a 'Civil-Military Fusion', a term coined in this century reflects the progressive mindset of that generation.

**Strategic Culture: Integration of Military in the Society.**

The Ahom Dynasty of Assam had a unique social structure with a strong military orientation, known as the 'Ahom Military System'. The society was organised around a military-centric structure, emphasising martial prowess and defence of the kingdom as paramount. The Ahom society had a rigid social hierarchy with the *Gohain* (Nobles) heading administrative units, followed by various military and civil officials, and then the commoners or *Paiks*.

- **Ahom Higher Defence Organisation/Higher Organisation.**[6] The highest functionaries of the Ahom state constituted the Patra-Mantri (Cabinet Ministers responsible for handling correspondence and communication). This group consisted of five individuals who also had the power to decide the succession to the throne. The administrative and military role of these noblemen were deeply enmeshed and accordingly they were trained and equipped. The Ahom King was known as *Swargadeo* (God of Heaven) with supreme powers of the state including the right to capital punishment. He was not an automatic heir like that of contemporary dynasties in the subcontinent but was selected by the cabinet from the male members of the royal family. In fact, there were a total of seven royal families earmarked during that time from where the king was selected, and the final selection was based on merit. The king also had to follow the rules of the process strictly. Any misuse of his prerogatives was considered a disgrace, resulting in penalties of disposal or death. The breakdown of the cabinet, an important factor in the growth of the dynasty, which was involved in strategic planning, is depicted in Figure 1.

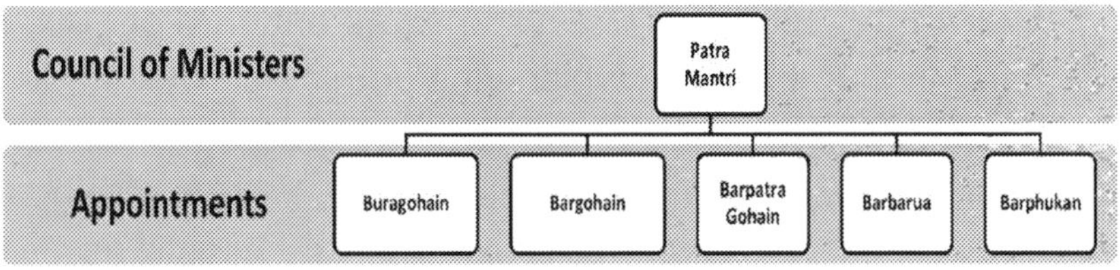


**Figure 1**

❑ **Nobles**. The upper echelons of Ahom society were composed of nobility and were primarily administrators who also held appointments as military officers of senior rank. This class was known as the *Gohain* and included various ranks such as *Swargadeos*, *Borpatrogohain* (Chief Guardian) and *Borgohain* (Chief *Gohain*) etc. This upper stratum of nobility mostly came with 'Ahom Lineage', but their appointments were based on elections or on merit and skill set. The middle level administrators or officers came from various backgrounds as well as lineage and were elected based on eligibility and merit.

❑ **Paiks**.[7] The Ahom society was divided into a system called *Paiks*, where individuals were categorised into clans, with each clan responsible for trained manpower for military service. It was this system which provided the government the much-required manpower for military, public administration, labour for infrastructure development etc. Every able-bodied man was trained in basic soldiering skills. It was a unique concept which provided the kingdom the trained peasant-soldiers who served the government at the time of emergency or hostilities. The *Paiks* were required to provide military service only when needed and also engage in agricultural and other activities during peacetime. This unique system of medieval era helped the Ahom King maintain a balanced Army with a reservist cadre and a productive population for economic prosperity. This system played a crucial role in the socio-economic success of the Ahoms for several centuries. This system was unheard of specially in the Indian mainland which was dominated by the Mughals, Sikhs, Rajputs and Marathas during this period, who had large standing armies which were a huge drain on the economy. The system was extremely successful as it brought about a strategic culture in the society and the commoners were the driving force behind the military success of the Ahoms over the Mughals. The system ensured that commoners had specific roles within the Ahom society, both in terms of military and civilian duties. The hierarchical organisation of nobility and commoners contributed to the functioning of the state, with each group having well-defined responsibilities. It helped in maintaining order, ensuring defence, and supporting the agricultural and economic activities of the kingdom. The organisation of the Paik system allowed the Ahom state to efficiently mobilise resources and manpower for various purposes, contributing to the kingdom's stability and longevity. Commoners were categorised into different groups based on their obligations and services to the state. The group names or titles are still being used as surnames in modern Assamese Society. The hierarchy within the higher organisation of the Ahoms and the *Paik* system of the commoners was a very good mix of family tradition, lineage, and merit-based system.

- **Decentralised Administration.** The Ahom kingdom had a decentralised administrative structure, with each region having military commanders responsible for governance including law and order as well as defence of the kingdom. These governors were adequately empowered with military components, legal and administrative powers. The nation's security remained paramount under these federal heads, driving a concerted effort that involved all sections of the society/whole-of-nation approach (another term coined recently, but part of Ahom strategic culture). Similar federal structures were not existing in the mainland and, therefore, very unique to the region. These have been adequately documented by the scholars who accompanied the Muslim invaders during that era.[8]

❑ **Military Tactics: Defensive Lines and Use of Terrain**. The Ahoms were masters of defensive battles. They had mastered the art of night fighting and guerilla warfare, which gave their defensive tactics an offensive flavour. There are multiple accounts by Persian historians mentioning the fear they instilled in the minds of the Mughal Army, which had repeatedly attacked the northeastern part of our country with limited or no success. The Ahoms were not the proponent of fortress warfare like the Marathas, Sikhs or the Rajputs. They fought their battles like the modern era armies. They used to employ *Paiks* to build fortifications (earthworks) to protect important towns, business establishments etc, which were more like bunds in alignment with natural obstacles, mostly water bodies. The Ahoms held these defensive lines with strength and used them to channelise the enemy into killing zone. The Battle of Saraighat is an extraordinary example of this strategy, wherein Lachit Borphukan and Atan Buragohain neutralised the Mughal flotilla at the sharp river bend of Brahmaputra just north of present-day Guwahati and their infantry and cavalry were dissipated at their camping grounds with multiple raids originating from the hilly areas and fortifications in the region.[9]

## Conclusion

The Ahom military system or militarised structure was instrumental in the dynasty's ability to withstand external pressures and maintain its rule for centuries, making it a distinctive feature of Northeast Indian history and culture. Before the Ahoms came into the Brahmaputra valley, the entire region was quite unorganised, with multiple chieftains and small rulers, who were more of administrators with limited sensitivity towards national security. In fact, the region was divided into tribal and non-tribal territory. The most important achievement of the Ahoms was the integration of these tribal non-tribal territories and bringing in a nationalistic approach towards security and sovereignty, a strategic culture which is there for all to see, admire and emulate. Unveiling the legacy of the Ahoms is like discovering a treasure trove of wisdom waiting to be shared with the world. Their rich tapestry of culture, governance, and innovation, holds invaluable lessons. There is a need to dive into the depths of history and resurface with pearls of wisdom for inspiration and guidance. It is time to dust off these forgotten chapters and weave them into the fabric of modern military culture, transforming ancient knowledge into contemporary inspiration.

## End Notes

[1] Prof SK Bhuyan, *Lachit Borphukan and His Times* (pg 166), published in 1947.

[2] Mr Gaurav Das, *How Bihu Became a Symbol of Assamese Identity*, Times of India 12 April 2017

[3] Ms Nasrin Ara Rehman, *Status of Women under the Ahoms: A Historical Study* (thesis submitted by Ms Nasrin Ara Rehman for her PhD from the Univ of North Bengal).

[4] Ms Tinamoni Rajkumari, *Trade Relation with the Frontier Region in The Ahom Period and the Administrative System*, JETIR June 2019, Volume 6, Issue 6

[5] Shehabuddin Talesh, *Tarikh-e-Aasham (1663)*, Translated from the original Persian by Mazhar Asif, Guwahati University

[6] Prof SK Bhuyan, *Atan Buragohain and his Times*, Lawyers Book Stall (published in 1957)

[7] Dr Jaysagar Wary and Bijit Brahma, Bodoland University Kokrajhar, *Paik System: A Machinery of Ahom Rule for 600-year,* Turkish Online Journal of Qualitative Inquiry (TOJQI), Volume 12, Issue 8, July 2021: 2926-2935

[8] Shehabuddin Talesh, *Tarikh-e-Aasham (1663)*, Translated from the original Persian by Mazhar Asif, Guwahati University

[9] Nilotpal Gohain, *Essay on Lachit Borphukan – "Assam's Hero who Halted the Mughals" (Pg 71-78)*, Edited by Rajib Handique and Wasbir Hussain, published by Govt of Assam (Nov 22)

# Section 2

## *Multi-Domain Warfare Perspectives*

# 6

# Multi-Domain Operations: A Reality Check

**Major General Sandeep S Sharda, SM, VSM**

**Abstract**

*Warfare doctrines ebb and flow, mirroring the prevailing anxieties of their eras. Some endure, instigating lasting reforms that shape history, while others are swiftly abandoned with the departure of their proponents. Some quietly recede into obscurity as their valuable insights melt into established practices, while their flawed notions are replaced by fresher ideas. The concept of 'Multi-Domain Operations' (MDO), evolving since 2016, stands at a crossroad, poised to follow any of these trajectories. This article provides a comprehensive exploration of MDO, examining its theoretical underpinnings, practical critiques, real-world applications, challenges in the Indian context, strategies for advancement and concluding reflections. It offers a critical assessment of the concept, dissecting key challenges and limitations. The Russia-Ukraine War a case study for MDO, analyses how both sides have employed multi-domain strategies to pursue their objectives. It further delves into the unique operational and strategic challenges faced by India in implementing MDO. Finally, the article outlines strategic pathways and actionable recommendations to address the identified challenges to propel India towards effective MDO implementation. The article synthesises the key insights and reflections presented throughout, reaffirming the significance of MDO in navigating the complexities of modern warfare. It underscores the imperative for continued innovation, collaboration and adaptability to meet the evolving security challenges of the 21st Century.*

## Introduction

Multi-domain Operations (MDO) represent a paradigm shift in military strategy, reflecting the reality of modern warfare's multi-dimensional nature. The concept emphasises the need for militaries to operate seamlessly across land, sea, air, space, cyberspace and cognitive domains simultaneously. It involves the synchronised application of capabilities across multiple domains to create synergies and exploit adversaries' vulnerabilities. It aims to overcome the traditional domain-centric approach by recognising the interconnectedness of modern conflicts and leveraging capabilities across all domains to achieve strategic objectives. The MDO is a United States (US) military concept that has undergone a doctrinal evolution from the 'Active Defence' strategy of the Vietnam War to the 'Air Land Battle' doctrine. This doctrine was the initial integration of dual domains, which later evolved into the Air Sea Battle concept, incorporating space and cyberspace alongside the traditional domains of air, land, and sea. Perhaps it was the development and progress of China's 'Unrestricted Warfare' that led the US to invest in the development, assimilation and ultimately the deployment of MDO.

While MDO offers promising opportunities for gaining strategic advantage and achieving mission success, its operationalisation presents a myriad of challenges. There is thus a need to understand the complexities associated with operationalising MDO, exploring integration difficulties, command and control complexities, technological vulnerabilities, training requirements and the need for an adaptive doctrine.

## MDO: A Critique

- **Generalisation of War**. Like one of its predecessor concepts, 'Effect Based Operations', the MDO concept too seems to have generalised warfighting. Any doctrine to be effective must recognise that war is inherently chaotic, unpredictable and violent (causing body bags). It is essentially a test of wills of two or more adversaries. Any attempt to apply forces in a mechanical manner is bound to fail. Attrition will happen; a fact now very well known to the main protagonists of the Russia-Ukraine and Israel-Hamas wars.

- **Lack of Clarity and Coherence**. The concept of MDO suffers from ambiguity due to the excessive use of adverbs and adjectives, making it difficult to grasp. It is often criticised for being laden with 'Buzzwords', which obscure rather than clarify the concept. The prevalence of vague language and generalities has influenced its formulation.

- **Optimism vs Reality**. The concept spans strategic, operational, and tactical levels, encapsulating almost all functions of the state, i.e., a 'Whole-of-Nation Approach'. However, integrating this approach into existing political and military frameworks may encounter resistance, as it implies a dominant or coordinating role for the military over other governmental ministries or departments. Moreover, inter-service competition can impede efforts to institutionalise MDO, which necessitates unified military forces. Furthermore, variations in service procedures related to training, budgeting and procurement hinder joint initiatives by constraining implementation within service-specific channels.

- **Technology Availability**. Much of MDO predicates on seamless communication and niche-technologies to achieve desirable synergies to exploit the enemy's vulnerabilities. In reality, despite a significant amount of attention in recent years, the level of assured connectivity is far from realistic. This assumption of technological maturity may be a fatal flaw in the concept, especially if the adversary possesses advance electronic warfare capabilities.

- **Span of Control**. With its all-pervasive view of conflict and whole-of-nation approach, it would be safe to assume that field commanders will have a rather difficult job to do, in controlling the n number of factors and forces at play.

## Russia-Ukraine War: A Case Study for MDO?

Recognising the context-dependent nature of warfare, the Russia-Ukraine war should not be interpreted as entirely predictive of what India may experience in a conflict with its adversaries. However, the ongoing conflict provides a compelling case study. This short analysis explores how both sides have employed strategies across land, sea, air, cyberspace and information domains to pursue their objectives in the conflict.

- **Land Domain**. In the land domain, conventional military operations, irregular warfare tactics and hybrid strategies have been employed by both sides. However, the ascendency of precision fires through long range vectors, enabled by pervasive surveillance, has stood out in the past two years of the war. Russia and Ukraine have struggled to conduct combined arms manoeuvre at scale, rendering them more vulnerable to the re-emergence of defence as the stronger form of warfare.

- **Sea Domain**. The maritime domain has also played a role in the conflict, particularly in the Black Sea region. Russia's annexation of Crimea provided it with control over strategic naval bases, enabling it to project power and assert dominance in the region. The Black Sea has witnessed naval manoeuvres, blockades and maritime patrols, impacting the flow of goods and resources to and from Ukraine. On the other hand, Ukraine has used a blend of surface and sub-surface sea drones, controlled through satellites to strike back at Russia.

- **Air Domain**. Russia and Ukraine have leveraged various air and missile systems; such as military and commercial satellites, Unmanned Aerial Vehicles (UAV) for Intelligence, Surveillance and Reconnaissance (ISR) and kinetic effects. Fixed-wing and rotary-wing aircraft have played a less significant role than many assumed they would, as both Ukrainian and Russian ground forces have denied air superiority to each other. The role of the UAV has been particularly prominent. Russia and Ukraine have used military and commercial drones to spot adversary forces and to direct massed and precision artillery fire. Both militaries have employed UAVs with lethal capabilities, such as Ukraine's use of the US made Switchblade loitering munitions and Russia's waves of Iranian Shahed-136 drones.

- **Cyberspace and Information Domains**. Russia has used cyber operations as part of its larger campaign against Ukraine. These operations were consistent with a so-called thunder run strategy intended to stoke chaos, confusion and uncertainty. In the cyberspace and information domains, both Russia and Ukraine have engaged in propaganda, disinformation campaigns and cyber-attacks to shape public opinion, influence perceptions and undermine each other's capabilities. Cyber-attacks targeting critical infrastructure, government systems and media outlets have been reported, highlighting the importance of information warfare in the conflict.

While both militaries leveraged each of the domains, there is little information to suggest that they conducted MDO in the manner that the concept is being expounded (probably since MDO is a recent construct). However, in the past year, Ukrainian forces with support from North Atlantic Treaty Organisation, have engaged in cross-domain manoeuvres during the ongoing conflict. Although these manoeuvres have been sporadic, they have highlighted the potential for MDO on the modern battlefield. The

Ukrainian theatre has become highly lethal due to ISR efforts and the devastating impact of targeting fires. Detection capabilities in the cyber domain and electromagnetic spectrum have further exacerbated the situation. Initially, Russian forces amassed with easily detectable signatures, created cross-domain vulnerabilities. Specifically, their ground forces were susceptible to kinetic attacks due to electromagnetic exposure. Ukraine astutely exploited these vulnerabilities by targeting fires. Notably, the high mobility artillery rocket system strike on a Russian troop dormitory in Makiivka resulted in significant casualties. Additionally, Ukraine executed a cross-domain fire operation to sink the Moskva, which served as the flagship of Russia's Black Sea Fleet. In summary, their experience underscores the importance of cross-domain synergy and manoeuvrability in shaping military strategies on the contemporary battlefield.

## Challenges: Indian Context

Operationalising MDO in the Indian context presents several challenges, reflecting the diverse geopolitical landscape, military capabilities and strategic imperatives. Some key challenges include:

- **Terrain and Geopolitical Complexity**. India's vast and diverse terrain, including mountainous regions, deserts, plains and coastal areas; presents unique challenges for conducting MDO. India's borders are characterised by various geopolitical dynamics, including long-standing disputes with Pakistan and China, as well as maritime challenges in the Indian Ocean region.

- **Integration of Military Services**. Achieving seamless integration and coordination among the Army, Navy, Air Force and other specialised units is crucial for effective MDO. However, historical service contentions, bureaucratic structures and differing operational doctrines can hinder interoperability and jointness.

- **Technological Modernisation and Interoperability**. All three services are in the process of modernising their equipment and capabilities, but challenges remain in achieving interoperability among diverse platforms and systems across different domains. Integration of emerging technologies such as cyber, space and unmanned systems requires significant investment and coordination.

- **Civil-Military Coordination and Whole-of-Government Approach**. Effective MDO require coordination not only among military services but also with other government agencies and stakeholders. Achieving a whole-of-government approach, involving coordination with ministries responsible for diplomacy, intelligence, law enforcement and disaster response, is essential but challenging.

- **Cyber and Information Warfare Challenges**. The evolving nature of cyber threats and information warfare presents significant challenges for MDO implementation. India faces cyber threats from state and non-state actors, necessitating robust cybersecurity measures and strategies to protect critical infrastructure and networks.

- **Human Resource and Training Requirements**. Developing a skilled and adaptable workforce capable of executing MDO is critical. This requires investment in training programs, joint exercises and professional military education to enhance cross-domain expertise, decision-making and leadership at all levels.

- **Budgetary Constraints and Resource Allocation**. With a galloping economy, budgetary constraints in true sense may not be a concern; however, prioritising investments in areas critical for MDO while balancing other defence requirements would be a significant challenge.

- **Logistical Challenges**. Ensuring effective logistics support across multiple domains and diverse terrains is crucial for sustained operations. India's vast geographic expanse and challenging terrain pose logistical challenges, including transportation, supply chain management and infrastructure development.

- **Adversarial Threats and Asymmetric Warfare**. India faces a range of adversarial threats, including hybrid and asymmetric warfare tactics employed by state and non-state actors. Addressing such threats such as terrorism, insurgency and proxy warfare requires adaptive and flexible multi-domain responses.

- **Cultural and Organisational Challenges**. Cultural factors, organisational hierarchies and bureaucratic processes within the armed forces can hinder the agility, synergy and innovation required for an effective MDO. Overcoming entrenched mindsets and fostering a culture of jointness and innovation is essential.

- **Long-Term Strategic Planning and Adaptation**. MDO requires long-term strategic planning and adaptive capabilities to anticipate and respond to evolving threats and emerging technologies. India's security establishment must continuously assess and adapt its strategies, doctrines and capabilities to maintain a competitive edge in the multi-domain environment.

## Breaking the Barrier: Way Ahead

Addressing these challenges requires a comprehensive approach involving strategic planning, policy reforms, technological innovation, organisational restructuring and capacity-building efforts tailored to specific geopolitical contexts and national security objectives. It will require concerted efforts from political leadership, military establishment, civil society and private sector stakeholders to develop holistic solutions and build resilient capabilities for MDO. Some strategies to address these challenges are given below:

- **Jointness and Interoperability**. There is a need to promote jointness and interoperability among the Indian Army, Navy, Air Force and other specialised units through joint training exercises, interoperable equipment procurement and integrated command structures. The anticipated theatre commands would achieve this synergy, which is sine-quo-non for prosecution of MDO. Moreover, joint exercises like the recently held Exercise Bharat Shakti demonstrate their interoperability and readiness for combat scenarios.

- **Technological Modernisation and Integration**. It is imperative to invest in technological modernisation across all domains, including cyber, space and unmanned systems, to enhance capabilities for MDO. Integrated systems and networks should be developed to enable seamless communication, data sharing and command and control across domains. Creation of Defence Cyber Agency in 2019 marked a significant milestone in efforts to strengthen cybersecurity posture. Concurrently, the move towards creating a dedicated Defence Space Agency is indeed a right one, as the necessity to protect assets and interests in space intensify, being the next arena for geopolitical competition. Headquarters Integrated Defence Staff thus plays a crucial role in coordinating technological modernisation efforts and integrating systems and networks for seamless command and control across domains.

- **Training and Professional Development**. It is important to enhance training and professional development programs to build cross-domain expertise, decision-making skills and leadership qualities among military personnel. A precursor to this could be the institution of a Joint Higher Command

Course to develop strategic thinking, collaborative leadership, and joint operational planning skills. There is also a need to foster a culture of collaboration and mutual support across service branches. Towards this end cross-billeting of staff officers is a step in the right direction, that needs a much-delayed impetus.

- **Civil-Military Coordination and Whole-of-Government Approach**. It is crucial to foster closer coordination and cooperation between the military and other government agencies, including ministries responsible for diplomacy, intelligence, space, cyberspace, law enforcement and disaster response. Mechanisms need to be developed for information sharing, coordination of efforts and joint planning to achieve common objectives. The entire exercise could be kick started with a National Operations Room manned by requisite staff from concerned ministries. Regular joint exercises and tabletop simulations can also be conducted to practice coordination and enhance readiness for various scenarios.

- **Resilience against Hybrid Threats**. It is vital to strengthen national resilience mechanisms to counter hybrid threats, including cyber-attacks, disinformation campaigns, and economic coercion. Cybersecurity capabilities should be enhanced to invest in critical infrastructure protection and promote public awareness and education on emerging threats. There is a need to work with technology and media companies to enhance transparency, improve content moderation practices, and combat the proliferation of fake news and propaganda.

- **Strategic Communication and Public Diplomacy**. It is imperative to implement effective strategic communication and public diplomacy strategies to shape perceptions, counter disinformation, and build public support for MDO efforts. Domestic and international stakeholders should be engaged with to convey India's strategic objectives, promote transparency and strengthen partnerships.

- **Long-Term Planning and Adaptation**. A long-term perspective should be adopted in planning and decision-making to anticipate and respond to evolving threats and challenges. There is a need to regularly foresee and assess India's strategic environment, technological advancements and emerging trends to adapt strategies, doctrines and capabilities accordingly.

- **Policy Reforms**. Policy reforms must be implemented to streamline defence procurement processes, enhance bureaucratic coordination, and promote innovation and agility within the defence establishment. This could be the make-or-break factor for all the future endeavours in national defence including MDO.

- **National Capacity Building**. There is a need to build an institutional capacity through investments in research and development, talent recruitment and organisational restructuring to support MDO implementation. *Atma Nirbhar Bharat* (Self-reliant India) needs to build on its initial successes into a cyclical process to obviate technology coercion during crisis.

- **Trial Project**. Commencing a trial project now is crucial to grasp the authentic challenges involved in establishing an MDO environment in the Indian context. Currently, the discourse on MDO remains largely theoretical in seminars or articles like these, which are primarily guided by western literature. Through the trial project, one can identify the requisite technologies, optimum organisational structures, and financial resources needed. A cost benefit analysis could then be carried out to adopt the most suitable course of action.

## Conclusion

The future of MDO holds both opportunities and challenges. Emerging technologies, evolving threat landscapes and geopolitical dynamics will continue to shape the way warfare is approached. Continued investment in innovation, collaboration and adaptability will be crucial for meeting the complex demands of future conflicts. By adopting strategies outlined earlier and implementing concerted efforts across strategic, organisational, technological and policy domains, India can effectively address the challenges of operationalising MDO and enhance its capabilities to meet the complex security challenges of the 21st Century.

7

# Roots of Contemporary Grey Zone Warfare in Indian History

**Colonel Kunal Sharma**

**Abstract**

*Grey zone tactics have been in vogue since the history of warfare itself. Ramayana, Mahabharata, the powerful and charismatic rulers in Indian history characterise India's true military psyche; whenever it was felt necessary, Kootneeti (Strategy) was also adopted. Kautilya's Arthashastra is identified as the 'Formative' ideational strategic text which is assessed to illuminate Indian strategic culture and strategies of war including* Koota Yuddha *(Asymmetric Warfare) and* Tusnim Yuddha *(Silent Fighting). These strategies still remain relevant and remain as the guiding factors towards nation building and all forms of warfare today.*

## Introduction

'Grey Zone' warfighting methodology has become popular in recent times because of two significant factors; deniability and low economic and human cost vis-à-vis conventional wars, which motivate nation states to adopt the practices of grey zone warfare. While Pakistan brings asymmetric threats through terrorism, China engineers multi-pronged cyber and non-contact warfare threats to target the networks. Beijing has resorted to pressure point tactics, face-offs and salami slicing at the northern borders besides leveraging its economic strength to adversely influence economic growth.[1] China's actions under grey zone warfare involve the ingress attempts along the northern borders in Doklam and Galwan, precluding the use of firearms to prevent any escalation, crafty use of maps and old fabricated revenue documents to reinforce their claims over territories and prompting Nepal to raise the Kalapani-Lipulekh dispute. Chinese grey zone campaigns target specific vulnerabilities in economic, military, geopolitical, cyber, information operations and legal domains.[2]

Pakistan realised that the spiralling cost of conventional war could only be compensated through hybrid warfare. It resorted to unconventional methods to carry out disruption through use of proxies, insurgents, espionage, cyber dis-information, historical half-truths, diplomacy and economic manipulation to avoid the impression of a military aggression. In the past, it has orchestrated terrorist attacks in Jammu and Kashmir, Mumbai (26/11), Uri and Pulwama, plane hijacking, Sikh insurgency, aid to insurgents in Northeastern states and fake currency and narcotics flow in India. Pakistan derives its strength from the 'Quranic Concept of War' announcing India as their traditional adversary.[3]

**Image 1**

The Modern Hybrid Warfare Doctrine in Russia was introduced by General Valery Gerasimov, the Chief of the General Staff. The Gerasimov Doctrine has blurred the lines between the polarised states of 'War' and 'Peace' introducing a kind of analogue to the Western idea of an intermediate continuum or grey zone. The doctrine, a mix of hybrid and threshold warfare, has also been termed as 'Hybrid Balancing'.[4] Three major components of the doctrine are the whole-of-government approach to warfare, fusing elements of hard and soft power across multiple domains and the idea of grey zone. Russia's grey zone tactics during Crimea's split from Ukraine brought success through bloodless annexation and overthrowing Viktor Yanukovych, Ukraine's Pro Russian President.[5]

However, the study of Indian military campaigns indicates multiple instances wherein grey zone tactics had been in vogue, albeit in different forms such as *Koota Yuddha* (Asymmetric Warfare), *Tusnim Yuddha* (Silent Fighting) and Guerrilla Warfare. In the *Ramayana*, *Hanuman* after having studied how the Lankan forces and defences were laid out, decided to make his presence known to the enemy so that he could dissuade *Ravana* of the future consequences of defeat. According to *Krishna* in the *Mahabharata*, war could not be won by mere bravado, chivalry and rigid codes, but it called for clever means against the mighty *Kauravas* with the ultimate aim of achieving victory. Kautilya in 350-275 BCE wrote extensively in the *Arthashastra* (Economics) regarding the means of orchestrating silent wars and concealed wars through diplomacy, spreading disinformation and discord amongst the kings.[6]

**Image 2**

## Application of Grey Zone Warfare in Indian Historical Context

The Epics, *Ramayana* and *Mahabharata* represent a model struggle between good and evil–both reckoned not as white and black but with shades of grey. Various incidents and case studies in both the epics are indicative of the fact that even during those times grey zone's success depended upon patience and an ability to covertly blend all the instruments of state power such as diplomacy, information, military, and economics. This study examines the dynamics of grey zone warfare by analysing its conceptualisation in the 'History of Bharat'.

**Influence Tactics in *Ramayana*.** *Hanuman* decided to psychologically frighten *Ravana* by allowing himself to be captured so that he could be produced before *Ravana* and have a direct dialogue to threaten him of the consequences by showing his strength.[7] However *Ravana* was too rigid for agreement and subsequently as the anxiety increased in *Ravana's* camp on reports of the giant *Vanara* (Monkey) force and the building of a causeway across the sea, *Ravana* assigned his confidants *Rakshasa* (demon) commanders *Suka* and *Sara*, the clandestine mission of estimating the strength of the *Vanaras* army. They disguised themselves by wearing 'Totem Symbols' like monkeys and pretended to be part of *Vanara* army. However, *Vibheeshana* discovered their disguise, and they were presented before *Rama*. Subsequently *Rama* pardoned

Image 3

Image 4

them and deliberately gave them all the details and showed them the strength of their army. He knew that they would narrate it back to *Ravana* and instil fear in his mind.[8]

**Exceptions of Code Violations in *Mahabharata*.** In *Mahabharata*, the great strategist and tactician that *Krishna* was, he directed the *Pandava* forces with professional genius to victory at every crucial juncture of the war. While *Bheeshma* advocated '*Dharam Yudha*' (A Righteous War) which was the direct approach, *Krishna's* doctrine of war preached the indirect approach or *Koot Yudha*. According to *Krishna's* concept, war could not be won by mere bravado, chivalry and rigid codes, but it called for down-to-earth means of *Kootneeti* (Strategy), with the ultimate aim of achieving victory at the end of the day. Whether it was creating an artificial sunset to provoke *Jaidratha* to come out, so that *Arjuna* could kill him or spreading disinformation of the death of *Ashwathama*, to demoralise and kill his father *Dronacharya* or fielding *Shikhandi*, the eunuch warrior against *Bheeshma*. During all these instances, the exceptions of violating the code were operational imperatives.[9]

**Battle of the Hydaspes**. In 326 BC, Porus fought against Alexander with 200 war elephants in his army. Alexander's Greek soldiers had never encountered elephants in battle. This had caused a scare amongst them and they suffered heavy casualties. However, Alexander's military genius overcame both the floods and the elephants and won a decisive victory over Porus. Subsequently, he decided to move further eastwards towards the *Magadhan* Empire. At this moment,

**Image 5**

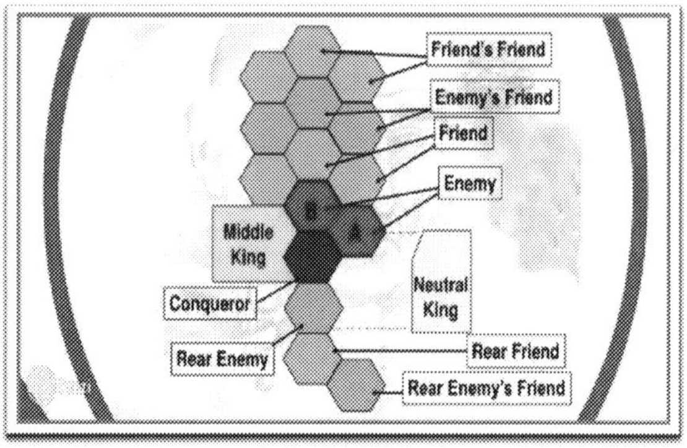


Image 6

*Chandragupta Maurya* visited the camp of Alexander and it is considered that he played a major role in demoralising the Greek soldiers with stories about the prowess of 6000 war elephants of the *Magadhan* army beyond the Beas River eastwards. It is pertinent that his mentor, *Chanakya* in his treatise, *Arthashastra*, writes about the need to demoralise the enemy before battle is joined.

***Kautilya's* Strategies of War.** It must be appreciated that *Arthashastra* was conceived by *Kautilya* for the *Vijigishu* (Victorious King), to establish a powerful empire encompassing the whole of India. On the concept of war, *Kautilya* underlines that "He who possessed a strong army and who has offered remedies against all threats, may undertake an open fight; if he has secured a position favourable to himself; otherwise a *treacherous fight is better to defeat the enemy".* The theory of *Mandalas* (Circle) and the *Kootneeti* are meant to help the victorious king to shape his 'Foreign policies and the intelligence setup' in such a manner so that a let-up therein did not render it vulnerable to a crafty neighbour. Nor does it presuppose that the conquering king will ever be at war with all his neighbours. With most neighbours, the interstate relationship gets resolved under the *Neeti* (Policy) conjunctions, rather than resorting to war, which caters for the worst scenario. The basic approach to foreign alliance and coalition was based on a concentric ring of natural adversaries and allies. Those in the immediate neighbourhood were to be considered potential enemies, ever ready to exploit one's weaknesses. The ones beyond and adjacent to it were the natural friends, being the enemy of an enemy. Thus, the concentric rings covering the state falling beyond and adjacent to ones neighbour's neighbour, constituted a source of remote danger of allying with your immediate enemy. Furthermore, if the theme character of the *Arthashastra* did not look beyond his frontiers, armed with an exhaustive intelligence network, how could he have dreamt of establishing the mighty Maurya Empire besides evicting the Greeks? Only a discerning and enterprising *Chandragupta* could have created the historical niche of being the greatest emperor of India.[10]

**Kautilya's Assessment of Threats.** Kautilya classified the national threats as; threat of external origin and internal abetment; internal origin and external abetment; external origin and external abetment and internal origin and internal abetment. Of these, he counsels that the internal danger ought to be eliminated on priority, for it is the internal danger, like a lurking snake, that is more serious than the external. Kautilya's classic counsel is, "If the threat is from an equally powerful or stronger enemy, avoid it by broaching a bargain or deal, and seeking alliances with neutral states". The endeavour should be to delay war until conditions are favourable, through extensive war preparations, winning over allies and large-scale operations by own *Gupatchars* (Spies) during the interim period, till one is fairly confident of a positive outcome in war. He further urges that against a collusive threat from the enemy and his allies, the main war effort should be directed to defeat the main enemy, with only a holding action against its allies. In a situation, where the appreciation indicates parity between the gains and losses after war, Kautilya propagates peace, for the costs of war are much too heavy in terms of the loss of manpower and destruction of national resources.

**Kautilya's *Kootneeti*.** The essential elements of the grey zone warfare advocated in *Arthshastra* are *Saam* (Persuasion), *Daam* (Rewards to allies and coercion to adversaries), *Dand* (Punishment), and *Bhed* (Division). The starting point of the *Neeti*

**Image 7**

is to win over the other person through *Saam*. On its failure, graduate to the policy to *Daam*, which may make headway. If both fail, take recourse to *Bhed*, which implies 'Divide and Rule' through intrigue in the opponent's camp. After having effectively used *Bhed*, the appropriate use of *Dand* is prescribed. It points to giving warning, snapping earlier treaties and declaring war when warranted. An amplified version of the *Arthashastra* policy contains seven elements of *Niti* as *Dana* (Charity), *Bheda*, *Maya* (Guile), *Upeksha* (Overlooking), *Inderjal* (Straragem) and *Danda*.

**Maharana Pratap, the Legendary Warrior.** In 1567 AD, when Akbar laid siege on Chittor, Rana Udai Singh, the then ruler of Mewar, decided to fight from the hills. Earlier, Rana Sanga too had displayed a marked flexibility in adopting guerrilla warfare against the larger Mughal forces. Guerrilla warfare was proven to be a judicious option to take on the mighty Mughals, by Udai Singh and his able successor Maharana Pratap. In the fabled Battle of Haldighati, Maharana's contingent of 20,000 comprising of cavalry, infantry and the light-footed *Bhils* (Tribes), who were adept in guerrilla warfare, fought with courage and bravado against 80,000 gigantic force of Mughals led by Man Singh of Amber. Although the battle ended with the defeat of Maharana Pratap, however he escaped and continued to fight guerrilla warfare from the south, not giving the Mughals a lull in battle. With the unyielding fierce campaign, the indomitable Rana ultimately attained the upper hand, and was able to recover all of Mewar except Chittor.

**Architect of the Maratha Empire.** Shivaji's most outstanding achievement was to weld together the Marathas, in the teeth of opposition of great powers, namely the Mughal Empire, Bijapur and the Portuguese. As a military genius, he based his war strategy on surprise and deception. Against a strong enemy, Shivaji would withdraw to hilly terrain to wage guerrilla warfare, and where it suited the purpose, he would press on with fighting the conventional set-piece battles. One of the most thrilling episodes of Chhatrapati Shivaji Maharaj was during the Battle of Pratapgarh, wherein Shivaji conquered and killed the cunning Afzal Khan, using intrigue and raw courage.[11] Another distinctive feature of Shivaji's strategy was the dynamic use of forts. Unlike the traditional use of forts, as nuclei of defence alone, he made greater use of these as pivots for launching offensive operations, to inflict attrition and disruption on the enemy.

**Image 8**

**India's Strategic Culture**. In the *Ramayana* and *Mahabharata*, the powerful and charismatic rulers in Indian history characterise India's true military psyche, in which exceptional strategies have been demonstrated during the acts of exemplary heroism, personal morality and fair governance; and whenever it was felt the *Kootneeti* was also adopted. Kautilya's *Arthashastra* is identified as the 'Formative' ideational strategic text to illuminate Indian strategic culture and strategies of war. These strategies still remain relevant and guiding factors towards nation building and all forms of warfare today.

## Way Ahead for India: Recommendations

Countering grey zone warfare involves a combination of proactive measures to deter adversaries and resilience-building to mitigate the impact of such tactics.[12] The various lessons derived from the glorious battles fought in Indian history by the great rulers provide relevant lessons even today and strategies to counter the threats in the present times also.

The future wars will be volatile, uncertain, complex and ambiguous, driven by information and evolving technologies. Accordingly, the efforts to prepare modular, agile and leaner forces are already underway in India for conflicts of the future. The victory markers for a nation as guided by the teachings of *Ramayana*, *Mahabharata*, Kautilya and Shivaji, Angre and Maharana Pratap to counter the grey zone warfare are as under:

- **Grand Strategy**. The Kautilyan theory of state clearly envisions its end goal and optimally employs all resources available to achieve it. The term 'Grand Strategy' is inclusively understood to mean the combination of national resources and capabilities, military, diplomatic, political, economic, cultural and moral, that are deployed in the service of national security.[13] Kautilya deals with the concept of grand strategy as a central theme of his treatise, incorporating each of the above mentioned factors, which demands for formulation of a national security strategy.

- **Whole-of-Government Approach**. The grey zone war requires the whole-of-government approach to deal with it. The response should be based on the principle of unity of efforts, simultaneity, integration and synergised approach.

- **Threats in the Grey Zone to be Responded in the Grey Zone**. The response requires a strategy and synergy between military and non-military partners and other law enforcement agencies.

- **Mixed Tactics Design**. A mix of above-mentioned tools such as diplomatic, cyber, informational, economic, political, asymmetric and military must be employed concurrently. The idea is that the operational commanders cannot achieve strategic objectives solely through military action but must address multiple domains across the enemy's territory to achieve appropriate goals.

- **Conventional Deterrence**. Although the armed forces will continue to be involved in dealing with the sub-conventional and hybrid threats at multiple levels, however, the conventional deterrence needs to be maintained at all times.

**Informationalisation and Multiple Domains Capability**. Cyber and information warfare capability need to be orchestrated under the realms of the grey zone continually. Social scientists, cyber experts and info warriors force must continue to fight the 'Battles of Minds' to protect systems and networks from the adversaries.

## Conclusion

Grey zone conflicts have changed the notion of warfare and the present security situation in India faces a new and evolving nature of conflict of grey zone warfare that teethers between war and peace. The absence of international laws and norms that govern the manifestation of grey zone conflicts makes the situation more complex. Therefore, there is a need to invest in new technologies and capabilities through whole of nation approach to counter the grey zone threats in the same arena.

> "*War in 21st Century is conducted at a roughly four-to-one ratio of non-military and traditional military tools and tactics.*"
>
> —*General Gerasimov, Chief of General Staff, Russia*

## End Notes

[1] CLAWS. Issue Brief No 198: Greyzone Conflict & Informationaization in Indian Context: Challenges Capabilities and Way Ahead by Poshuk Ahluwalia

[2] Grey Zone Threats: Implications on Force Structuring by Lt Gen Dushyant Singh (Retd)

[3] India in the Middle.of Greyzone Warfare by Col Rajinder Kushwaha (Retd)

[4] Velery Gerasimov's Doctrine by Alexander Giles, p 14

[5] Corelation of military and non military measures: Velery Gerasimov's Doctrine by Alexander Giles

[6] Kautilya's. Arthashastra on War and Diplomacy in Ancient Indiaby Roger Boesche

[7] Indian Military Thought : Kurukshetra to Kargil & Future Perspectives by Brig K Kuldip Singh (Retd), p 54

[8] Ibid, p 58

[9] Ibid, p 81

[10] Kautilya's Arthashastra Indian Strategic Culture and.Grand Strategic Preferences by Dr Kajari Kamal

[11] https://organiser.org/bharat/how-chhatrapati-shivaji-maharaj-defeated-afzal-khan-the-tyrant

[12] https://www.indiandefencereview.com/chinas-grey-zone-warfare-indias-response/

[13] Kautilya's Arthashastra Indian Strategic Culture and Grand Strategic Preferences by Dr Kajari Kamal

# 8

# Counter Unmanned Aircraft Systems: Indian Context

**Colonel Apratim Sharma**

*"F-35 Joint Strike Fighter will likely be the last manned strike fighter aircraft the Department will ever buy or fly, and that autonomous unmanned vehicles will be the new normal in ever-increasing areas".*

*—Ray Mabus, United States Secretary of the Navy*

**Abstract**

*The History of war is replete with instances wherein a nation that has effectively and innovatively harnessed technology has been victorious. Innovation with information stems revolution in military warfare and the current world order is witnessing an acute and swift uprise in the military warfare through the employment of Unmanned Aircraft Systems (UAS) - which is the modern world's game changer in cross-border military operations. Proliferation of UAS, due to inherent advantages, is evident in modern conflicts. Thus, it is imperative for modern forces to possess Counter UAS (C-UAS) capability to combat UAS evolution. This article has a hawk eye lens on the future roles of UAS; analyses its tactical, operational and strategic impact; assesses their vulnerabilities and having ascertained the need for C-UAS in future wars; suggests C-UAS philosophy, methodology and plausible approach in Indian Context.*

## Introduction

Modern conflicts have witnessed metamorphosis in exploitation of air as the means of manoeuvre space, to define outcomes. Combat Drones are the element of transition, employed across the spectrum of warfare from 'No War No Peace' to 'Full Spectrum War'. Armed Unmanned Aircraft Systems (UAS) have emerged as the next generation threat to combat forces in conventional as well as non-conventional domains,[1] alongside impacting the 'Hybrid and Grey Zone Warfare'. 'Drone Warfare' is outlining the consequences of recent conventional Russia-Ukraine Conflict (RUC), Israel-Hamas conflict between a nation state and non-state actors and Yemen's Houthi rebels disrupting the Red Sea shipping thus prompting the United States (US) and Britain to counter attack Houthi's. Rise of drones has found easy access amongst nation-states, Non-State Armed Actors (NSAA) and terrorists due to high efficacy, cost benefit advantage and deniability calculus, taking sophisticated air and Air Defence (AD) systems by surprise and revealing operational limits during Nagorno-Karabakh and the RUC. As a result, more than 102 countries and non-state actors operate Drones.[2] Modern warfare is a technology-driven 'Cat and Mouse Game' wherein, Counter-UAS (CUAS) are evolving to counter the 'Threat of the Decade'.

Reckonable UAS threat subsists in Indian context, with adversaries having acquired armed UAS capabilities through indigenous innovation, collusivity or friendly draws, like combat-proven Bayraktar TB2, Akinci etc. Thus, developing and possessing potent CUAS capability is an imperative for Indian security calculus to mitigate hostile UAS risk to own mobile, semi static and static assets.

**Image 1: Evolution of Unmanned Aerial Platform;** *Source: JAPCC*

## Understanding UAS

Technically, a 'Drone' refers to any vehicle which can travel on its own in water, land or air.[3] Most of the military literatures use the terms like remotely piloted aircraft, unmanned aerial vehicle, Unmanned Combat Aerial Vehicle (UCAV) etc, which reflect the way the technology has matured. However, internationally accepted term in military operations is UAS, as promulgated by the US Federal Aviation Administration in the 2000s. UAS comprises everything that makes an unmanned aircraft work like its Global Positioning System (GPS) module, ground control module, transmission systems, camera, software and ground controller. On 12 Mar 2021, the Indian Government adopted the term UAS, published vide official Gazette 'Unmanned Aircraft System Rules'.[4]

## UAS: Threat and Risk Conundrum

The threats from unmanned operations have risen exponentially and there are huge risks if this threat is not countered effectively. A study of hostile UAS (2016) by the Remote Control Project, Oxford Research Group[5] defines threat as:

$$\textit{Threat} = \textit{Capability} \times \textit{Intent}$$

$$\textit{Risk} = \textit{Likelihood (Threat + Vulnerability)} \times \textit{Impact}$$

A threat is an actor possessing both capability and intent to attack. A risk is a function of a threat, vulnerability and likelihood of the threat attacking the vulnerability and the potential impact of the attack.

Current RUC epitomises this equation. Ukraine acquired the UAS capability to thwart another Russian misadventure, akin to 2014. When Russian vulnerabilities were exploited the impact was detrimental for the Russian AD and Air Force. Over the last decade US, China, Russia, Turkey and Iran have considerably advanced UAS development and recently even the small island nation, Maldives acquiring the most advanced Byrakhtar TB2. Due cognisance is necessitated, with the Northern and Western adversaries being in possession of huge UAS range and inventory. The UAS is the most pronounced contemporary 'Multi-domain Battlefield Weapon' and presents unique challenges.

**Image 2:** *Source: www. icpsnet.org*

**Threat Matrix**. UAS threat is likely to manifest in three military domains as under:

- **Strategic**. Threat manifestation in this domain is still distant and requires advanced technological skill. The objective shall be to impact cognitive domain of enemy to disrupt application of forces. A possible leverage of disruptive technology viz. robotics, Artificial Intelligence (AI) and collective (cloud-like based) intelligence, network communications, internet of things etc in future may manifest this future projected threat to reality, with state actors being the prime operators.

- **Operational**. Threat manifestation is primarily from human controlled/semi-autonomous UAS, using communication links from satellites and be carried out by State actors. For eg., in Jul 2014, Russia destroyed four Ukrainian Army brigades preparing to conduct a cross-border attack through UAS surveillance. Contrarily, in the current RUC nearly two dozen Russian naval vessels have been damaged/destroyed by Ukraine, like Tsezar Kunikov, Moskva, Olenegorsky Gornyak, Novocherkassk etc.[6] Non-state actors would take several more years to acquire such technology due to its niche nature and the cost factor.

- **Tactical**. UAS employment in this domain is an imminent threat and may manifest from Small UAS (sUAS)/improvised hobby drones as swarms, exploiting weaponised devices against service personnel, ammunition dumps, leadership etc by terrorists. In the last decade, easy availability, proliferation, cost effectiveness and local innovation of UAS by NSAA has changed the equation of force application. Non-state groups, including Islamic State of Iran and Syria (ISIS), Hezbollah, Hamas, Jabhat al-Nusra and Ansar-Allah (Houthi Movement) have demonstrated sUAS/Drones capability for a wide range of operations including aerial reconnaissance, surveillance, strikes and propaganda. Few instances are, Hezbollah employed Mirsad-1 Drone in Nov 2004 to carry explosives over Israel, ISIS employed over 300 commercial off the shelf and homemade drones during Iraq and Syria operations (2014) and recent chemical tanker (Chem Pluto) attack by Iranian drones in the Indian Ocean, on 24 Dec 2023.[7]

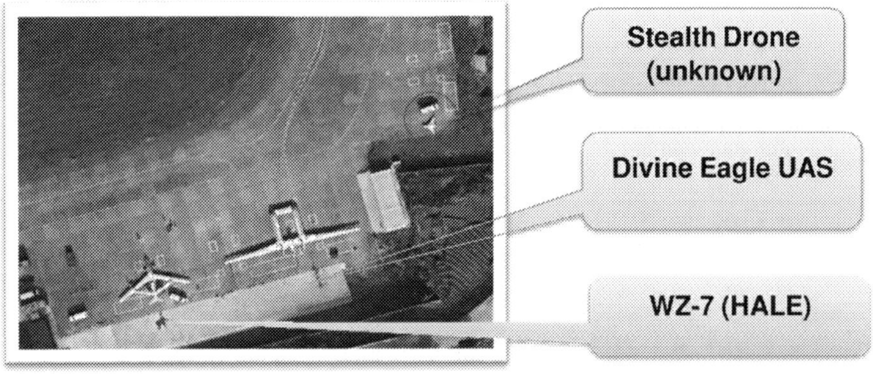


**Image 3: AWAC UAS: Divine Eagle;** *Source: https://twitter.com/foolsball/status*

An updated photo of Guizhou Aviation Industry Corporation apron, Anshun Huangguoshu Airport taken on 27 Nov 23, is seen to have parked WZ-7 High Altitude Long Endurance (HALE), Divine Eagle Airborne Warning and Control System (AWACS) UAS and an unrecognised stealth drone.[8] Offensive drone power of China is listed below in Table 1:

| Type | Role/Capability | Inventory/Payload | Remarks |
|---|---|---|---|
| | • Fuselage diameter– 1.2 to1.5 m<br>• Fuselage height to length ratio of 1:12<br>• Length-4.4 m to 18 m<br>• Wingspan-40-50 m | • Seven Active electronically scanned array radars<br>• Airborne moving-target indication and Ground moving-target indication radars - track air and surface targets<br>• Synthetic aperture radar-Ground target's images | • Largest AWACS UAS<br>• Can track stealth aircrafts like F-35 |
| **HALE** | • Altitude ceiling >30,000 ft<br>• Endurance > 48 hrs | • EA 03<br>• WZ-7 | Offensive Drone |
| **Medium Altitude Long Endurance** | • Altitude ceiling 10,000-30,000 ft<br>• Endurance 24-48 hrs | • BZK 005<br>• GJ 1<br>• GJ 2 | |

| Type | Role/Capability | Inventory/Payload | Remarks |
|---|---|---|---|
| **Wing Loong-II (WL-II)** | • Combat radius–4000 km<br>• Endurance–20 hrs<br>• Service Ceiling–5000 m<br>• Speed–370 kmph | **Payloads**<br>• Rockets-AKD10, GB 10<br>• Bombs-FT series 7.9, 10<br>• Anti-ship missiles - YJ9E<br>• Air-to-ground missiles - YZ212, BA7<br>• Laser guided cluster bombs YJ 102A<br>• Anti-radiation missiles and precision guided munitions | • Advanced Strike UAS<br>**Operations**<br>• With manned platforms<br>• Independent strikes |
| **Tianying/ Skyhawk** | • Speed- up to 200 kmph<br>• Endurance-6 to12 hrs | | • Strike UAS |
| **WZ-8** | • Supersonic intelligence, surveillance, target acquisition, and reconnaissance platform | | |
| **Gongji 11** | • Combat radius - 1000km | | |

**Table 1**

## Implications

Critical implications for India are:

- Chinese rotary as well as fixed wing drone swarms' capability provides flexibility and ease of operations, even in hostile terrain of the northern borders.
- Open source intelligence reports confirm drone swarm exercises involving hundreds of drones in swarms, practicing precision attacks in autonomous mode.[10.]
- The Divine Eagle UAS, with its long range anti-stealth capabilities and X/ultra-high frequency band radars, is force multiplier in both offensive and defensive operations.
- People's Liberation Army Air Force can quickly intercept stealth enemy aircraft, missiles and ships by using Divine Eagle as an AWAC picket.

## Adversarial Threat: Pakistan

Pakistan invigorated the drone program (2009) with its first indigenous drone, Burraq, designed to carry a 50 kg payload and up to 200 km range.[11] Pakistan claims to possess fourth-largest drone arsenal in the world. Moreover, Pakistan's UAS threat comprises proxy threat from her all-weather friends too.

**Image 4: Akinci;** *Source: www.icpsnet.org*

Salient Pakistan's UAS capabilities are are given in Table 2 below:

| Type | Role/Capability | Inventory/Payload | Remarks |
|---|---|---|---|
| **Burraq UCAV** | • Range–1000 km<br>• Altitude ceiling–500 m<br>• Endurance-12 hrs | **Payloads**<br>• Bombs -YC 200<br>• ASM - AR-1 and Barq ASM laser-guided missile[12] | • Strike UCAV |
| **Chinese Wing Loong**[13] | • Combat radius- 4000km<br>• Endurance- 20h<br>• Service Ceiling- 5000m<br>• Speed 370km/h | • 48 × Wing Loongs - 2018 deal<br>• Four × Wing Loongs (2020)-China Pakistan Economic Corridor and Gwadar Port safety<br>• Four×CH4 akin to Wing Loong | • Strike UAS |
| **Bayrakhtar TB-2** | | **BARQ Laser-Guided ASM**<br>• Weighs 47.5kg<br>• High explosive warhead Range–08 km[14] | |
| **Bayraktar Akinci (Flying Fish)**[14] | • Body length -12.5m<br>• Height-4.1 m<br>• Wingspan-20 m<br>• Maximum Take-off Weight - 4.5 tons<br>• Powered by - pair of turboprop engines | | • Oct 22-Operator training in Turkey<br>• Apr 2023 - received 1st batch |
| **Anka** | | | • Co-produced with Turkey<br>• Turkey's most advanced drones. |

**Table 2**

## Implications

The implications are:

- **Regional Security**. Pakistan's drone program poses a serious threat to South Asia's regional security especially India.
- Pakistan can use UAS for:
    - **Kinetic Operations**. Attacks on military and strategic targets, for e.g., Drone attack on Jammu Airfield.
    - **Non-kinetic Operations**. Small drones are frequently in use for smuggling of counterfeit currency, drugs, small arms and ammunition across the porous borders across Shakargarh Bulge.
    - **Long-Range Precision Strikes(LRPS)**. To reduce close combat on battlefield and avoid human losses along with maintaining deniability, UAS can be exploited for LRPS.

**UAS Manifestation: RUC**. Ukraine effectively used Matrice 300/ Mavic-3 for recce and US Switchblade-300 and Bayrakhtar TB-2 for offensive strikes. Contrarily, Russian Orlan-10 was less effective for reconnaissance and Shahed-136 was used for strikes. Novel drones with propulsion systems using jet skis from Canada were involved in the attacks in Sevastopol.

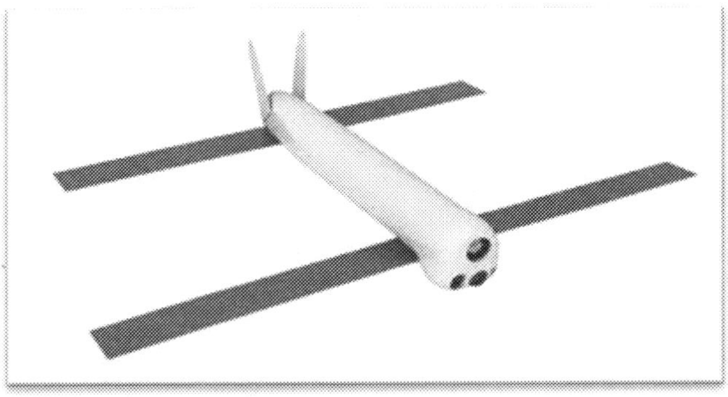

**Image 5: Switchblade Drone**

*Source : https://techland.time.com/2012/11/01/best-inventions-of-the-year-2012/slide/the-switchblade-drone/*

## Future Roles/Exploitation

The UAS can be utilsed in the future for:

- Automatic target detection, recognition and destruction.
- Electronic attack.
- Nuclear payload delivery.
- Combat search and rescue.
- Offensive and defensive counter air.
- Refuelling, aerial delivery/resupply of ammunition and medicines.

## Overall Assessment: UAS Threat

The overall UAS threat assessment is as under:

- Armed Forces are certain to develop and exploit autonomous drone swarms into new operational concepts and doctrine before 2035.
- Advances in Machine Learning (ML) and quantum computing will advance drone swarms operational concept.
- Disruptive technologies shall relegate single human operating single platform to a level of irrelevance.
- NSAA/Terrorist Groups will extensively exploit UAS.
- UAS exploitation will be pronounced in the escalation matrix.
- RUC demonstrated the need for indigenous capability development and need for robust strategic partnerships.

## C-UAS Threat

**UAS Counter Measures**. C-UAS platform is a system capable of lawfully and safely disabling, disrupting or seizing control of UAS.[16] Unique challenge in C-UAS lies in its application as per potential scenario. The counter measures differ in peacetime to that of combat; even between those faced in a terrorist incident, insurgency and peer-on-peer warfare.[17] For example, a peacetime

UAS attack shall primarily attract non-kinetic response to avoid escalation, while kinetic response shall be prudent in conflict.

**C-UAS Methodology**. C-UAS technology is used for securing the airspace around critical Vulnerable Areas (VAs)/Vulnerable Points (VPs) and high value targets in three distinct phases:

- **Detection and Tracking Phase**. Sensors detect, locate and track incoming UAS threat in relation to the coordinates of a VA/VP. Sensors employed are high sensitivity radars, passive Radio Frequency (RF) sensors, Electro Optical-Infra Red (EO-IR) cameras and acoustic sensors.
- **Identification and Decision Phase**. Data from multiple sensors is synthesised and positively identified/classified prior to interdiction decision.[18] Identifying the threat and decision making is the key command and control function.
- **Interdiction Phase**. This amplifies the range of effects, to include UAS landing/activating 'Return to Home' mode (jamming/spoofing), complete/partial destruction (lasers, projectiles, impact drones, High-power Microwaves (HPMs) etc).

**C-UAS Effectors**. Futuristic UAS technology necessitates integrated C-UAS platforms comprising Non-Kinetic and Kinetic effectors/techniques:

- **Soft Kill Techniques**. Following aim to make UAS operationally ineffective:
    - **RF Jamming**. RF link between UAS and operator is disrupted by generating RF interference, forcing UAS to either descend or return back/go rogue.
    - **RF Hijacking**. Entails electronically taking over UAS through data-link protocols and advanced software to break-in secure 256-bit encryption.[19]
    - **GPS Jamming**. It involves disrupting UAS satellite navigation link as was used to thwart the Organisation for Security and Co-operation in Europe Special Monitoring Mission to Ukraine in 2018.[20]

- **Spoofing**. Feeding spurious communications/navigation links to take control of UAS is spoofing and can be achievable with focussed technological capability. In 2011, Iran successfully captured a highly sensitive American RQ-170 Sentinel stealth UAS [21] intact.

❑ **Hard Kill**. Both non-kinetic and kinetic effectors are employed:

- **High Energy Laser**. Physical destruction caused by destroying/burning critical components.
- **High-power Microwaves**. High intensity microwave energy damages UAS electronics and is effective against swarms.
- **Nets/Projectiles**. Nets entangle targeted UAS to destroy/disable it.

**Image 6: C-UAS Nets;** *Source: Aerospace America*

- **Impact UAS**. A UAS is guided to collide with adversaries UAS. An integrated platform can have electronic system as first line of defence and a kinetic system as a backup.

## C-UAS Approach: Indian Context

**Indigenous Capability.** Contemporary indigenous C-UAS capabilities are:

- **Anti-Drone System (ADS).**[22] Defence Research and Development Organisation (DRDO) has developed an ADS**,** encompassing detection, identification and neutralisation of drones through soft and hard kill options, which was deployed during Independence Day 2020. It can detect and jam micro drones up to 3 km and target with laser up to 1-2.5 km.

**Image 7: Anti-Drone System;** *Source: www.economictimes.com*

- **Drone Guard System(DGS).**[23] BEL has developed DGS**,** configured to detect, track and neutralise intruding drones. It utilises RF spectrum for detection, EO-IR sensor to track and RF jamming to neutralise by hampering communication link as well as blinding its GPS source.

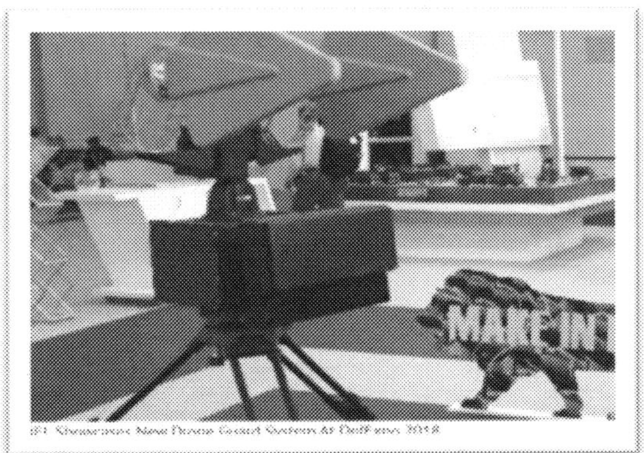


**Image 8: Drone Guard System;** *Source: www.defenseworld.net*

## Way Forward: Enabling Forces

To counter UAS threat and develop C-UAS capability, it's imperative to prepare a comprehensive roadmap involving all stakeholders, including government, lawmakers, security forces, scientific community and industrial workforce. An effective C-UAS setup in the Indian security calculus would require a timed roll-on plan, a comprehensive approach, technological, operational and strategic considerations, innovation, technology and Research and Development (R&D).

**C-UAS: National Strategy**. C-UAS threat will require synchronised, simultaneous and cohesive approach at national level:

- 'Whole-of-Government' approach is indispensable, essentially pertaining to regulations, indigenisation, innovation and Transfer of Technology (ToT).
- Comprehensive UAS guidelines for formulation and enforcing resilient and punitive regulations against illegal use of UAS.
- Strengthen association with the C-UAS industry who comprehend the threats and technological requirements.
- Easing regulations for micro, small, and medium enterprises to collaborate in developing C-UAS platforms.
- Conduct C-UAS conclaves for better ideation and sharing of vision and, thus, pursue technology and system development.
- Funding R&D in emerging technologies and C-UAS endeavours.
- Overseas collaboration with technology solutions through ToT.

**C-UAS: Recommended Structure**. Recommendations on implementing the C-UAS setup are:

**Strategic Aspects**

- **Strategic Planning**. Formulate long-term strategic C-UAS development program outlining objectives, scope and milestones through comprehensive threat assessment.

- **Unified Approach**. Establish effective coordination mechanisms among various government.

- **R&D**. Allocate substantial R&D funding, under '*Atmanirbhar Bharat Abhiyaan*' (Self-reliant India Mission), alongside establishing domestic and international research partnerships with institutions, universities and private companies to leverage expertise and resources. Invest in dedicated testing and evaluation facilities to assess the effectiveness of C-UAS technologies.

- **ToT and Joint Ventures (JV)**. Explore ToT opportunities with countries owning advanced C-UAS capabilities and facilitate JVs to accelerate technology adoption and knowledge exchange.

- **Training and Skill Development**. Develop specialised training programs and courses/certifications in C-UAS technology for military, law enforcement and relevant agencies.

- **Legislation and Regulation**. Develop and implement clear legal and regulatory frameworks. Address issues related to privacy, airspace regulations and the use of force in countering UAS threats.

- **Public Awareness Campaigns**. Launch public awareness campaigns to educate the public about potential risks of unauthorised drone activities.

- **Cybersecurity Integration**. Integrate robust cybersecurity measures into C-UAS systems and establish protocols for securing communication channels and data integrity.

- **Scalability and Upgradability**. Design C-UAS systems with scalability and upgradability to adapt to evolving threat scenarios and technological advancements. Ensure that the developed systems can accommodate future enhancements and modifications.

## Operational Aspects

- **Organisational Restructuring**. Follow 'Combined Arms Defence Concept'.

- **Integrated Approach**. AD setup to be reorganised to train and equip for C-UAS operations, integrating para military forces and central police organisations.

- **Asset Allocation**. UAS threat is omnidirectional necessitating detection and interdiction along the entire border, which is an expensive preposition. Apropos, a surveillance and engagement grid operating under the Joint Air Defence Centre (JADC) at Corps headquarters needs to be evolved. Hence, asset allocation and engagement orders, be it soft kill or hard kill, be exercised under positive control of JADC.

- **Technological Integration**. Invest and explore AI and ML for advanced threat detection algorithms.

- **Capability Development**. C-UAS technology is niche, expensive and possessed by developed countries. Apropos, indigenised capability development needs to be time bound:

    - **Short-term**. To procure niche detection cum interdiction systems which have been tested during recent conflicts (Ukraine, Syria, etc) with ToT as part of the deal.

- **Long-term**. Based on technical know-how gained from inductions, simultaneous focused development roadmap should kick start, integrating capability and efforts of DRDO, industry and users.

❑ **Integrated Multi-Layered Defence**. Device multi-layered defence structures to mitigate UAS threats, combining various technologies viz jamming, direct energy weapon and electronic warfare. Seamless integration of C-UAS systems into operations across all domains and levels of warfare.

❑ **Interoperability**. Interoperability and seamless integration with existing defence infrastructure through JADC be ensured.

## Tactical Aspects

❑ Evolve immediate and effective countermeasures against sUAS threat.

❑ Train forces on handling sUAS threat by preventive and available reactive countermeasures till C-UAS technology is made available.

❑ Procurement of low cost EO-IR sensors and non-kinetic effectors (both soft and hard kill) in Phase-1 and kinetic effectors (hard kill) in Phase-2.

## Conclusion

The ongoing RUC has demonstrated the need to ensure seamless integration of C-UAS systems into operations across all domains and levels of warfare (strategic, operational and tactical) to deter and deny critical space and strategic advantage to adversary, while at the same time ensuring the same for own forces. An efficient C-UAS in short term and an indigenous capability in long term, under *Atmanirbhar Bharat*, is the way forward for ensuring peace by ensuing deterrence and in case of any misadventure, ensuring victory.

## End Notes

[1] Andrea Bertolini, *Artificial Intelligence and Civil Law; Liability Rules for Drones* study, 13 December 2018, available at https:// www.europarl.europa.eu/ RegData/etudes/STUD/2018/608848/IPOL_STU (2018)608848_EN.pdf, accessed on 15 Nov 23.

[2] Dan Gettinger, The *Drone Databook.* 25 September 2019, available at https:/ /dronecenter.bard.edu/projects/drone-proliferation/databook accessed on 17 Dec 23.

[3] *What's the Difference Between Drones, UAV, and UAS? Definitions and Terms,* Pilot Institute, 22 March 2020, available at https://pilotinstitute.com/drones-vs-uav-vs-uas/ accessed on 17 Dec 23.

[4] Digitalsky.dgca.gov.in. *Unmanned Aircraft System Rules, 2021,* available at https://digitalsky.dgca.gov.in/assets/files/UAS Rules/ accessed on 17 Dec 23.

[5] Hostile Drones: The Hostile Use of Drones by Non-State Actors Against British Targets, January 2016, available at https://www.oxfordresearchgroup.org.uk accessed on 17 Dec 23.

[6] https://www.rferl.org/a/ukraine-navy-black-sea-russia/32826343.html accessed on 06 Feb 24

[7] livemint.com/news/world/pentagon-says-iranian-drone-attack-hit-chemical-tanker-near-india 11703378750741.html accessed on 20 Feb 24

[8] https://twitter.com/foolsball/status/1759973294176948574 accessed on 23 Feb 24

[9] https://www.popsci.com/divine-eagle-chinas-enormous-stealth-hunting-drone-takes-shape/ by Jeffrey Lin and P.W. Singer, 10 Jul 15 accessed on 15 Jan 24.

[10] https://www.vifindia.org/article/2022/october/17/the-future-of-ground-based-air-defence#_ accessed on 15 Jan 24

[11] https://southasiapress.org/2023/09/21/the-rise-of-pakistans-drones-how-they-are-changing-the-game-in-kashmir-india-and-the-south-asian-regionaccesed on 10 Jan 24

[12] The Future of Ground Based Air Defence | Vivekananda International Foundation (vifindia.org) accessed on 15 Jan 24

[13] The Future of Ground Based Air Defence | Vivekananda International Foundation (vifindia.org) accessed on 15 Jan 24

[14] https://southasiapress.org/2023/09/21/the-rise-of-pakistans-drones-how-they-are-changing-the-game-in-kashmir-india-and-the-south-asian-region accessed on 29 Feb 24.

[15] https://www.icpsnet.org/comments/pakistan-acquisition-of-turkish-drones-091023 accessed on 29 Jan 24

[16] Wang J, Liu Y & Song H, *Counter-Unmanned Aircraft System(s) (C-UAS): State of the Art, Challenges, and Future Trends,* IEEE Aerospace and Electronic Systems Magazine, Vol 36(3), March 2021, p. 4–29, available at https://doi.org/10.110/maes.2020.3015537 accessed on 20 Jan 24.

[17] Stephen W. Miller, *Fighting Back Against UAS,* Asian Military Review, Jun/July 2020, available at https://www.magzter.com/stories/ military-defence/asian-military review/ fighting-back-against-uas, accessed on 20 Jan 24.

[18] *Countering Threats from Unmanned Aerial Systems (C-UAS) - IEEE,* available at https://www.gov.uk/government/publications/crowded-places-guidance accessed on 29 Feb 24.

[19] Westbrook, Tegg, *"The Global Positioning System and Military Jamming: The geographies of electronic warfare,"* Journal of Strategic Security 12, no. 2, 2019, available at https://digitalcommons.usf.edu/jss/vol12/iss2/1 accessed on 29 Jan 24.

[20] Ibid.

[21] Scott Peterson, *Downed US Drone: How Iran Caught the 'Beast',* Christian Science Monitor, 09 December 2011, available at https://www.csmonitor.com/World/Middle-East/2011/1209/Downed-US-drone-How-Iran-caught-the-beast, accessed on 29 Jan 24.

[22] *Independence Day: DRDO's Anti-Drone System,* available at https://economictimes.indiatimes.com/news/defence/independence-day-drdos-anti-drone-system-was-part-of-pm-modis-security-at-red-fort/drdos-anti-drone-system/slideshow/ 77558751.cms, accessed on 08 Feb 24

[23] BEL's Drone Guard: Def Expo 2018, available at https://www.aviation-defence-universe.com/bels-drone-guard-system-on-display-at-defexpo-2018 accessed on 29 Feb 24.

9

# Dominating the Invisible Battlefield: Manoeuvre Warfare in the Electromagnetic Spectrum

**Colonel Nirbhay Gautam**

**Abstract**

*Electro-Magnetic (EM) manoeuvre warfare is a concept based on agility and adaptability, similar to conventional warfare. It emphasises freedom of manoeuvre and swift adaptation within the EM environment to maintain information dominance over adversaries. This article explores the principles of manoeuvre warfare and how militaries employ the EM Spectrum (EMS). The EMS is not a domain itself but rather serves as the overarching environment within which military operations occur. It encompasses various domains, including sea, land, air, space and cyber. The military's use of the radio spectrum has intensified significantly since World War I and it is now nearly inconceivable to imagine military engagements without leveraging it. EM manoeuvre warfare leverages pre-emption, movement, tempo, dislocation, disruption and deception just like conventional warfare. Mastering manoeuvre warfare in the EMS is crucial for militaries as wars increasingly move into this domain. It requires not only technological prowess but also strategic thinking and the ability to outsmart the opponent.*

## Introduction

Field Marshal Montgomery's insight from World War II - "Losing the war in the air means losing quickly", remains valid today, extending beyond aerial warfare to include the Electromagnetic Spectrum (EMS), which has emerged as a critical battleground. Success in this modern realm, akin to traditional warfare, relies on Electro-magnetic Manoeuvre (EMM), a concept based on agility and adaptability. Martinsen, Pace, and Fisher emphasised in their influential 2014 work that 'Freedom of Manoeuvre' and swift adaptation within the Electromagnetic (EM) environment are vital for maintaining 'Information Dominance' over adversaries.[1] This article delves into the principles of manoeuvre warfare, exploring how militaries employ the spectrum and why it has become a competitive arena.

## Applicability of Conventional Manoeuvre Warfare Principles to the EMS

Before delving into the nuances of EMM, understanding the core principles of conventional manoeuvre warfare is imperative. Christopher Bellamy, a respected expert in maritime security, eloquently summarised it as the movement of forces on the ground to secure advantageous positions for defeating or coercing the enemy. Surprise, deception, and agility constitute the cornerstones of this approach, encompassing both physical and decision-making agility.[2]

Manoeuvre warfare revolves around creating dilemmas for opponents by manoeuvring forces into superior positions to achieve objectives. It acknowledges adversaries as thinking, reactive entities not mere targets. Strategist William S Lind echoes this sentiment, defining manoeuvre warfare as a comprehensive style of warfare characterised not only by positioning oneself well against the enemy but by surpassing them in speed and tempo, ultimately leading to victory.[3] This approach relies on key principles like pre-emption, movement, tempo, dislocation, disruption and deception, all aimed at securing an advantageous position over the adversary.

Leonhard highlights pre-emption as seizing opportunities before one's opponent, catching the adversary off guard. Like surprise, it hinges on the adversary not anticipating the move, thereby, providing a valuable advantage of seizing the initiative, either temporarily or permanently.[4] Rapidity and surprise are key tools, striking first, unexpectedly, can grab control before the battle even starts. However, merely taking the initiative is not enough, the same needs to be maintained. This is where manoeuvre warfare's other aspects come in. Movement is not just physical troop or weapon relocation but manoeuvring them to positions advantageous against the enemy. While related, tempo is not just speed, it is about completing tasks and missions faster than your adversary, maximising efficiency and impact. While speed refers to physical movement, slowing down the enemy mentally by interfering with their decision-making process can also provide a crucial tempo advantage. Whoever reacts faster sets the pace and controls the initiative.

Dislocation, as defined by the Oxford Learner's Dictionaries, means disrupting someone's organisation and normal functioning. Leonhard brilliantly calls it 'The art of rendering the enemy's strength irrelevant'. In other words, the adversary is inhibited from achieving its goals on its terms i.e., their preferred time, location or conditions. Both movement and tempo can create friction and hinder the adversary's operations. EMM warfare enables to engage, weaken or even destroy the adversary's Centres of Gravity (CsoG) without relying on direct physical attacks. Imagine the enemy relies on oil imports to fuel their war machine. Suddenly, ports, refineries and storage depots become critical targets for their CsoGs. These are the crucial points upon which their entire operation hinges. Similarly, if their communication hinges on just a few key exchange points, those too become CsoG. Striking these vital points creates dislocation, throwing adversary's plans into chaos.

Ultimately, the goal of manoeuvre warfare is victory with minimal cost, ideally without firing a single shot. It's about creating intricate dilemmas, pushing adversary to collapse from within, rather than simply grinding them down through attrition. It's about winning swiftly, efficiently and with minimal loss of life or resources.

## Military's Reliance on the EMS

The EMS plays a fundamental role across various conflict domains, encompassing sea, land, air, space and cyber. It is not a domain itself but rather serves as the overarching environment within which military operations occur. Dating back to the 'Big Bang', approximately 13.8 billion years ago, the EMS comprises all forms of EM radiation, notably encompassing radio waves, microwaves, light (including infrared, visible, and ultraviolet), and ionising radiation.

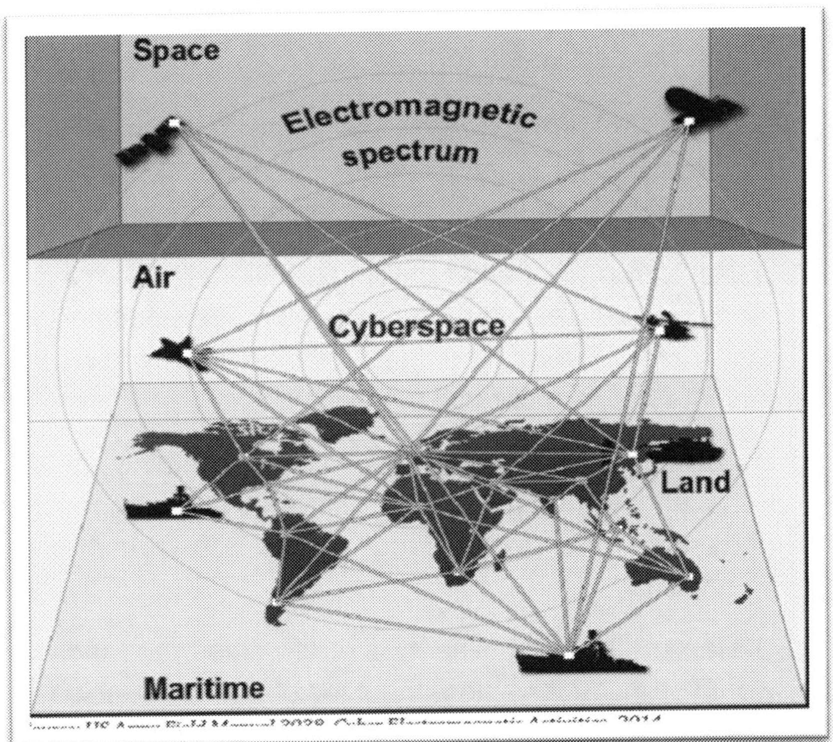


Image 1

The military's utilisation of the radio spectrum significantly intensified from the World War I onwards, particularly accelerating during the World War II with the widespread adoption of radar and radio communication technologies by all participating factions. This trend persisted throughout the Cold War era and remains prevalent in contemporary military operations. Indeed, military engagements without leveraging the radio spectrum in some capacity at tactical, operational, or strategic levels have become nearly inconceivable.

Imagine fighting a war across land, sea, air, and even space, without a shared communication network, navigation system or intelligence source. That is practically impossible, thanks to the radio spectrum, an invisible battleground older than war itself. This slice of the EMS, ranging from low-frequency radio waves to high-frequency microwaves, serves as the backbone for military operations. Soldiers use it for:

- **Communicating**. From transmitting tactical messages on the ground to facilitating satellite calls across continents, the radio spectrum serves as the backbone of global connectivity.
- **Navigating**. Whether utilising traditional radio navigation techniques or relying on modern global positioning system technology, determining one's location heavily relies on the intricate network of radio signals.
- **Gathering Intelligence**. Monitoring enemy communications and tracking their movements often necessitates accessing and deciphering information from the radio spectrum.
- **Radar**. Detecting enemy aircraft, ships, and individuals would be inconceivable without the utilisation of radio waves, which bounce back to disclose their precise locations.

- **Emerging Weapons**. This category encompasses not only the devastating EM pulse generated by nuclear explosions but also newer, non-nuclear directed energy weapons, underscoring the evolving role of radio technology in warfare.

## The Radio Spectrum as a Realm of Competition

The competition within the military realm of the radio spectrum is commonly referred to as Electronic Warfare (EW). EW encompasses any military action utilising EM and directed energy to either control the EMS or launch attacks against the enemy.

EW comprises three main components, Electronic Attack (EA), Electronic Protection (EP) and Electronic Support (ES). EA involves actions aimed at hindering or diminishing an enemy's effective use of the EM spectrum, such as jamming and EM deception. EP, on the other hand, focuses on safeguarding personnel, facilities and equipment from the adverse effects of friendly or enemy employment of EW that could degrade or neutralise friendly combat capabilities. ES entails actions directed at detecting, intercepting, identifying and locating sources of intentional and unintentional radiated EM energy for immediate threat recognition.

Increasingly, offensive and defensive military cyber operations are conducted in conjunction with EW. Cyber operations, defined as coordinated actions with a defined military purpose in cyberspace, often rely on the radio spectrum for execution. For instance, EA systems like jammers, designed to transmit radio signals into hostile radar or radio systems, can facilitate the delivery of cyber effects. For example, if a cyber-attack is targeting a hostile radar, malicious code may be transmitted via a radio signal to the radar's antenna. Similarly, it can be transmitted to a tactical radio used by enemy troops for voice and data communication. In both scenarios, the radio jamming signal serves

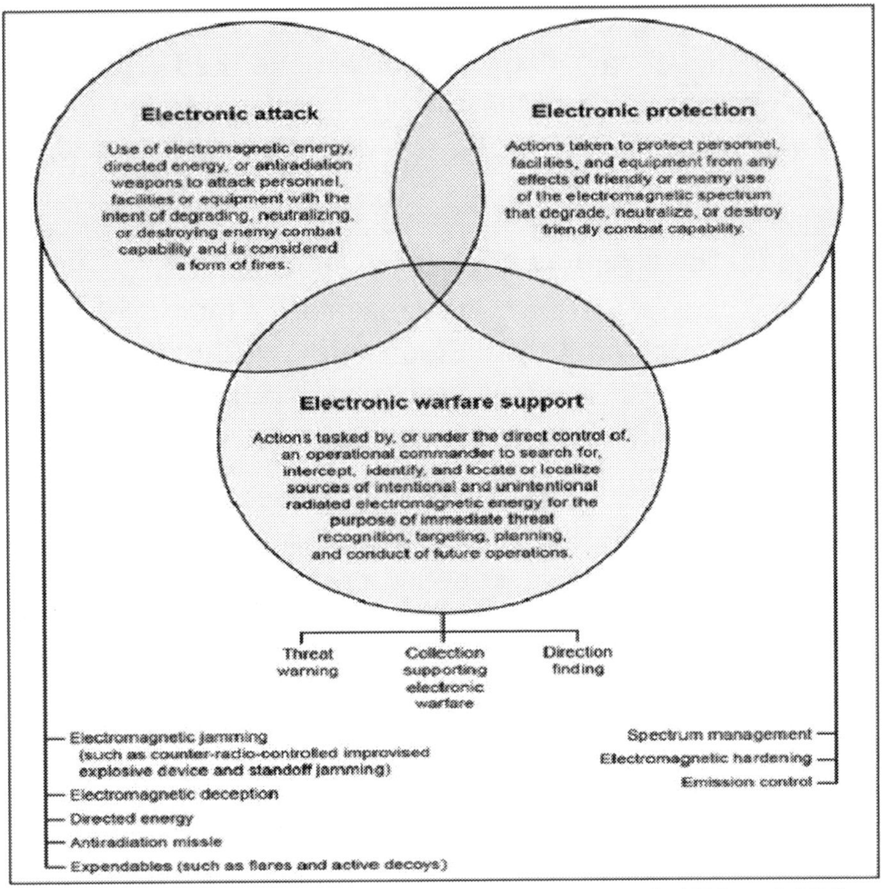


*Source: Cyberspace and Electronic warfare operations, U.S. Army Field Manual, 2017*

**Image 2**

as the conduit for introducing the cyber-attack into the radar or radio system.

The integration of EW and cyber warfare disciplines is evident in the development of Cyber and Electromagnetic Activities (CEMA) doctrines aimed at aligning these efforts. For instance, the United Kingdom Ministry of Defence's 'Joint Doctrine Note 1/18: Cyber and Electromagnetic Activities' underscores the importance of synchronising and coordinating cyber and EM activities to achieve operational advantages while denying adversaries' use of the EM environment and cyberspace.[5]

CEMA operations can manifest tangible effects in the physical realm. For example, a hypothetical CEMA attack targeting a hostile actor's land forces at a port aims to disrupt their deployment process. This attack would involve leveraging both EW and cyber effects. By transmitting malicious code on frequencies used by smartphones connected to the port's local mobile network, the attack overrides the port's cyber security and infects computers controlling its operations. Consequently, critical systems like floodlights may be disabled, causing chaos and delays in loading forces for deployment. This scenario illustrates how the fusion of cyber and electronic effects can significantly impact battlefield operations. Just like conventional warfare, EMM leverages pre-emption, movement, tempo, dislocation, disruption and deception.

### Pre-emption

Pre-emption can act like both defence and offence. In the 2008 war between Georgia and Russia, tensions had been simmering since the 2003 'Rose Revolution', in Georgia, which brought a pro-western government to power and triggered North Atlantic Treaty Organisation's interest in the country. Separatist activities in Georgia's South Ossetia region escalated, culminating in a Georgian military deployment on 07 Aug 2008. Russia responded with a full-scale invasion the next day. Cyberattacks against Georgia began in Jul, prompting the government to seek 'Cyber Refuge' by moving critical services onto servers in Estonia, Poland and the United States (US). This clever move ensured these services remained operational despite the attacks, essentially pre-empting further disruption. It also showcases not just pre-emption, but also a form of movement (repositioning services) to outmanoeuvre the cyber offensive.

## Movement and Tempo

If a military cannot pre-empt its adversary's actions within the radio spectrum, it can still endeavour to leverage the spectrum to make decisions more swiftly than its opponent. At its essence, the concept of movement and tempo in EMM warfare hinges on the speed at which one force progresses through the Observe, Orient, Decide, and Act (OODA) loop compared to the other. The OODA loop concept was pioneered by Colonel John Boyd of the US Air Force, based on his experiences in the Korean War. If the red force navigates the OODA loop faster and with better decisions than the blue force, it gains an advantage. Accelerating the red force's loop can be done by hindering the blue force's progress. This keeps the blue force reactive and the red force proactive. EW disrupts enemy communication, influencing the pace of loop navigation.

Nevertheless, the principle of the OODA loop entails more complexity than merely making decisions at a faster rate than one's enemy, these decisions must also exhibit superior quality compared to those of the adversary.

The emergence of cognitive radio and radar techniques looks set to fundamentally influence the impact of movement and tempo on OODA loop navigation. Cognitive radio and radar systems harness Artificial Intelligence (AI) to emulate human reasoning and problem solving.[6] AI software is integrated into these devices for this purpose. These cognitive methodologies could hold significant implications for military operations, aiding in the swift navigation of OODA loops compared to adversaries by assuming substantial portions of human decision-making. For instance, consider a scenario where a blue force radio comes under attack from a red force jammer. Traditionally, the radio operator would need to detect the jamming and manually adjust the radio's transmission behaviour to evade it. However, AI software utilised in a cognitive radio would be trained to recognise jamming signals and take corrective actions autonomously. Furthermore, the AI software would continuously learn from its surroundings over time. Similarly, a radar equipped with AI software would identify jamming attempts and respond accordingly. Employing cognitive methodologies could assist in preserving one's access to the spectrum within heavily contested EM environments.

However, what happens if both opposing forces employ cognitive systems? Does this negate any advantage? Much will hinge on how cognitive techniques are employed and the efficacy of their designs. Additionally, it will depend on the engineering, scientific, and innovative capabilities of those developing these systems. In the future, cognitive radars and radios will undoubtedly be developed, but their capabilities will not be uniform across the board.

## Dislocation and Disruption

While movement and tempo seek to exploit the radio spectrum as an arena in which to help accelerate one's own OODA loop navigation at the expense of one's adversary, dislocation works to render the enemy's strength as irrelevant.[7] The examples below will show how dislocation can precipitate disruption. Returning to dictionary definitions, disruption is 'The action of preventing something, especially a system, process, or event, from continuing as usual or as expected'.[8]

Dislocation forms part of the People's Liberation Army's (PLA) 'Systems Warfare' approach. This approach stresses the identification and targeting of vulnerable, critical 'System Components' within the hostile force.[9] In adopting this system's approach, the PLA is arguably embracing a Clausewitsian philosophy of targeting the enemy's CsoG. Hostile targets in the PLA systems warfare concept include red force sensors, communications networks and Command and Control capabilities.[10] The PLA embeds EMM into its thinking as such targets can be rendered ineffective by electronic and cyber-attacks, as much as they can by kinetic action.

A compelling instance of dislocation employed in EMM warfare unfolded in 2007 when the Israeli Air Force (IAF) targeted a suspected Syrian nuclear reactor in Dayr az-Zawr, eastern Syria. Prior to, during and after the attack, it was imperative to incapacitate the Syrian Integrated Air Defence System (IADS) to prevent it from engaging the IAF's aircraft. The IADS consisted of radars capable of detecting incoming planes and relied on radio networks to exchange information regarding Israeli aircraft, including their whereabouts, velocity, and altitude. This intelligence could be shared with other components of the IADS such as Surface-to-Air Missile batteries or fighter aircraft. Recognising Syria's IADS as a critical vulnerability that needed to be neutralised for the operation's success, the IAF embarked on this task.

This neutralisation was accomplished by the IAF through a blend of EW and cyber-attacks. These measures caused Syrian radars to malfunction during the raid, rendering them incapable of identifying and tracking the IAF aircraft. Consequently, the raid proved successful, resulting in the destruction of the suspected reactor. The assault on the Syrian reactor underscored the tangible, theatre-wide impacts that manoeuvring within the spectrum could yield. The disruption triggered by the cyber-attack hindered Syria's air defence systems from functioning normally, showcasing the potency of dislocation in this domain.

### Deception

Imagine feeding fake news to the adversary, leading it down the wrong path, that is the power of deception in the radio spectrum, directly impacting their decision-making. It will entail planting false information in their communication networks, scrambling their radars with fake signals or using special materials to make own planes and tanks 'Invisible' to radar. Imagine armies relying heavily on data flowing through radio and satellites. Disrupting those channels with clever 'Electronic Lies' can create chaos and give own forces a major advantage. But deception is not a solo act, it works hand-in-hand with other strategies like disruption and dislocation, creating a web of confusion and misinformation that leaves the adversary stumbling in the dark. As wars increasingly move into the EMS, mastering deception will be crucial.

**The Indian Canvas**

The Indian subcontinent, a crucible of complex geopolitical rivalries, has witnessed a paradigm shift in the character of warfare towards the invisible battleground of the EMS. Here, amidst the Himalayas and bustling megacities, nations are increasingly vying for dominance in this silent realm, employing the principles of manoeuvre warfare to gain an edge. Nations like India, Pakistan, and China are investing heavily in advanced EW capabilities, encompassing offensive and defensive tactics.

India's pursuit of EM dominance faces unique hurdles. Limited budgets, complex terrain and the rapid evolution of technology pose constant challenges. Additionally, navigating a complex regional environment necessitates a delicate balance between deterrence and cooperation. Collaborative information-sharing with regional actors is crucial to build trust and prevent accidental escalations. Furthermore, international treaties and norms governing cyber and electronic warfare are urgently needed to mitigate the risks associated with this unseen battleground.

While technology reigns supreme, the human element remains pivotal. Skilled personnel capable of strategising, adapting and executing complex operations within the EMS are indispensable. Investing in training and education becomes as crucial as acquiring hardware. Mastering manoeuvre warfare in the EMS is not just about technological prowess but also about strategic foresight, responsible development, and international cooperation.

Navigating the complex web of challenges and opportunities in this invisible battleground will determine India's future security landscape. Only by harnessing agility, innovation, and responsible engagement can India truly secure its position in the spectrum, ensuring peaceful coexistence in the region and beyond. Certain key postulates for a future roadmap are summed up as under:

- **Agile Spectrum Operations**. Develop agile spectrum management frameworks to dynamically allocate frequencies based on mission priorities. Utilise cognitive radio and software-defined networking to optimise spectrum usage while denying adversary's access.
- **Offensive Cyber Operations.** Employ cyber manoeuvre warfare techniques to penetrate adversary networks, disrupt command and control systems and degrade their ability to exploit the EM spectrum. Prioritise offensive cyber capabilities alongside traditional kinetic operations.
- **EW Integration**. Integrate EW platforms with manoeuvre forces to provide electronic support and electronic attack capabilities. Enable EW assets to rapidly reposition and respond to changing battlefield dynamics, denying adversaries the ability to establish dominance in the EM spectrum.
- **Fusion of Intelligence and Electronic Warfare**. Develop integrated intelligence and electronic warfare capabilities to provide commanders with real-time situational awareness of the EM battlespace. Fuse signals intelligence, electronic surveillance and cyber intelligence to identify and exploit adversaries' vulnerabilities.
- **Joint Interoperability**. Foster interoperability between the army, navy, air force and cyber command to synchronise operations across land, sea, air and cyberspace. Establish joint doctrine, training and exercises to enhance collaboration and coordination in EMM warfare.

- **Training and Education**. Invest in training and education programs to cultivate a cadre of EM warfare specialists. Develop simulation and wargaming exercises to simulate complex EM environments and refine tactics, techniques and procedures.

- **International Collaboration**. Engage in partnerships and alliances to share best practices, technologies and intelligence related to EMM warfare. Participate in joint exercises and interoperability initiatives to enhance collective defence capabilities.

## Conclusion

Manoeuvre warfare in the EMS represents a critical aspect of modern military strategy, leveraging technology and agility to gain strategic advantages. Through the utilisation of electronic warfare, cyber operations and information dominance, militaries can disrupt enemy communications, deceive adversaries and safeguard their own networks. This dynamic approach enables forces to exploit vulnerabilities, control the battlespace and achieve decisive victories with minimal casualties. However, as technology evolves, so do the challenges and complexities of manoeuvre warfare in the EMS. Continual adaptation, innovation and investment in capabilities will be essential to maintain superiority and ensure success in future conflicts.

## End Notes

[1] Thor Martinsen, Phillip E Pace and Edward L Fisher, 'Manoeuvre Warfare in the Electromagnetic Battlespace', Journal of Electronic Defence (Vol. 37, No. 10, October 2014), p. 32.

[2] Christopher Bellamy, 'Manoeuvre Warfare', in Richard Holmes (ed.), The Oxford Companion to Military History (Oxford: Oxford University Press, 2001), p. 541.

[3] Martinson, Pace and Fisher, 'Manoeuvre Warfare in the Electromagnetic Battlespace', p. 31.

[4] Robert Leonhard, The Art of Manoeuvre: Manoeuvre Warfare Theory and Air land Battle (New York, NY: Ballantine Books, 1991), p. 62.

[5] Development, Concepts and Doctrine Centre, 'Joint Doctrine Note 1/18: Cyber and Electromagnetic Activities', Ministry of Defence, February 2018.

[6] Tim Fountain and Leander Humbert, 'Improving the Capabilities of Cognitive Radar and EW Systems', 8 February 2022.

[7] Leonhard, The Art of Manoeuvre, p. 66.

[8] Cambridge Dictionary, 'Disruption'.

[9] Norman Wade, OPFOR Smartbook-1 – Chinese Military: Forces, Operations and Tactics

[10] Ibid.

# 10

# Airpower in the Grey Zone

**Air Marshal Anil Khosla, PVSM, AVSM, VM (Retd)**

*The Grey Zone is characterised by intense political, economic, informational, and military competition more fervent in nature than normal steady-state diplomacy, yet short of conventional war. It is hardly new, however, the cold war was a 45-year-long grey zone struggle in which the West succeeded in checking the spread of communism and ultimately witnessed the dissolution of the Soviet Union.*

*Unconventional Warfare in the Grey Zone*
*Joint Force Quarterly (1st Quarter, Jan 2016)*

**Abstract**

*Recent trends world over, indicate that national political objectives are increasingly being achieved by grey zone operations, without official declaration of war. The grey zone operations include multifarious forms of state sponsored activities that are being carried out in the metaphorical zone between war and peace, maintaining the threshold below that of conventional war. They are not limited to military domain and characterised by high degree of denial and ambiguity. The world at large and India are in a grey zone conflict scenario and are likely to remain in it for a long time. Airpower can play a major role and can effectively be utilised in many ways in these such operations. This requires a change in mind-set, organisational adaptation and some amount of capability enhancement, reorientation, and training. Finally, innovation and out of the box approach is essential to deal with grey zone situations and threats.*

---

This article was published in the USI Journal (Apr-Jun 2021)

## Introduction

In earlier days, states or nations used to resort to open armed conflicts by declaring war, with the aim of achieving an objective using force. Recent trends indicate that national political objectives are increasingly being achieved without official declaration of war. There are multifarious forms of state sponsored activities that are being carried out in the metaphorical zone between war and peace. These grey zone activities have become a norm in the recent years. The grey zone warfare is best defined as an aggressor engaging in actions that circumvent traditional norms and laws of war, in the pursuit of political strategic objectives. The grey zone conflict operations are unclear and ambiguous in character, and are orchestrated in such a way that the threshold is maintained below that of conventional war. These conflicts are carried out in any of the multiple domains, using variety of means as a weapon.

Air power, besides offensive use, can also be effectively utilised in many ways, in non-conventional hostile situations categorised above. Various aspects of grey zone operations need to be deliberated from the point of view of airpower involvement. A certain amount of reorientation would be required in application of airpower in these grey zone situations supported by capability enhancement in certain fields.

## Grey Zone Operations or Conflicts

**Definition**. Grey zone conflicts, also referred by some as shadow wars have been defined in many ways. They are not formal or traditional conflicts or full-scale wars between nations or states. If war and peace were to be given the shades of black and white, then grey zone operations or conflicts would fall somewhere in between the peace-conflict continuum. One of the definitions of the grey zone conflict is 'The contested arena somewhere between routine statecraft and open warfare'. Two major characteristics of grey zone conflicts are that the threshold is maintained below the level of full-scale war, and second that, the means of operations are not restricted only to military actions. Varieties of instruments of power, often asymmetric and ambiguous in character, are used to achieve the objectives.

**Means**. Grey zone conflicts focus on the weaknesses and the vulnerabilities of the countries being addressed. Aggressors use a hybrid approach to exploit their adversary's weaknesses through the use of diplomatic, informational, military, and economic instruments of power. The vulnerabilities could include weak economic conditions, internal disparities, ethnic alignments, and religious polarisation etc. Based on these vulnerabilities, local population, disillusioned elements or even the diaspora could be exploited. The grey zone activities could be in the domain of politics, economy, social movements, diplomacy, cyber, space, information, psychological and/or communications.

**Characteristics**. Grey zone operations are generally sub-conventional in nature employing irregular means. They could be overt or covert, carried out by proxy players or non-state actors. Ambiguity is essential to keep conflict in the space between peace and war, and the aggressors always endeavour to maintain a high degree of ambiguity and deniability. Invariably, these operations are conducted in multiple domains, at times using both kinetic and non-kinetic modes simultaneously. They generally include the nuances of other classifications of hostile actions like No-War-No-Peace (NWNP), hybrid operation, asymmetric and sub conventional warfare etc.

**Comparison/Differentiation**. Grey zone conflicts NWNP operations and hybrid warfare are terms, often used by security analysts and academics to describe prevailing hostile conditions between two countries. NWNP operations also fall in the same zone as grey zone conflict, but NWNP operations are generally referred to military actions, whereas, grey zone activities could be in any of the numerous domains mentioned above. Grey zone conflicts and hybrid warfare are other two terms which could be confusing. Grey zone is an operational environment encompassing the space between peace and war, whereas hybrid warfare is a strategy with reference to the threats and means that are exploited in multiple domains. These threats and means could either be employed in full-fledged open war or in grey zone conflict situations. At the same time, grey zone conflict and hybrid warfare are not independent of each other; they are intricately linked to each other.

## India's Grey Zone Threat Scenario

India is a large and the most diverse nation with two inimical neighbours. India's myriad problems provide innumerable opportunities for the belligerent adversaries to exploit in the grey zone. The increased radicalisation in the neighbourhood has further opened up new grey spaces. Grey zone tactics are being followed both by China and Pakistan using different means.

**Pakistan**. Pakistan is using the low-cost option of grey zone tactics against India by promoting violent extremist groups. These non-state actor groups get funding and training in Pakistan, to carry out irregular warfare against India. The spectrum of anti-India grey zone warfare emanating from Pakistan is wide ranging from disinformation and incitement to terrorism. The grey zone activities of Pakistan include propaganda, false narratives, cyber warfare, and encouraging internal dissent and terrorism, to undermine the Indian national security.

**China**. China is the master of grey zone operations. This type of warfare is embedded in her philosophy, strategic thoughts, and doctrines. China has further mastered the art of converting and using anything and everything into a weapon for grey zone warfare. China practices its famous three-warfare strategy, which encompasses non-kinetic means like psychology, media, and law warfare, to achieve political ends. China has been extensively using psychological warfare and coercion against India with the aim to subdue India without fighting.

**Dealing Strategy**. India, a large democratic and bureaucratic state is perceived to be a weak spot, ideal for grey zone operations. It will lose out if it does not adapt to the changing nature of warfare. India must prepare to deter China and Pakistan from extreme forms of grey zone aggression. An important part of any grey zone response strategy is to undertake institutional reform. These organisational and structural reforms, need to be embedded in the current structures, in a phased manner without causing too much of turbulence. A word of caution, a change for the sake of change due to peer pressure needs to be avoided. The change should be based on factors like threat perception, technological threshold, economic conditions and geopolitical environment. India must develop a framework of strategic deterrence to deal with grey zone warfare.

## Grey Zone Warfare Aspects: Relevance to Air Power

Grey zone operations comprise of many components and are waged in multiple domains and dimensions. These domains may be widely dispersed like land, air, maritime, cyber, space, and information. Based on the uniqueness of each situation, aggressors would determine in which domain, they can achieve the greatest leverage in the grey zone. The goal of using these domains would be to fuse multiple tactics and techniques together to strain the opponent's resources and taking advantage of his weaknesses. Cyber and information domains are the most fertile domains for grey zone operations. A look at likely activities in these domains is required from the point of view of airpower application and involvement, i.e., how do these activities directly affect instruments of airpower and how can airpower be employed against in these situations.

**Land Domain**. The social space is generally the incubator for ideology and political aspirations, and it provides the necessary ingredients for any uprising or rebellion. Fuelling and supporting insurgencies is the most common grey zone activity. This may include covert or overt support resorting to arming, funding, espionage, infiltration and/or subversion. Resorting to terrorism overtly by the non-state actors has become a norm these days. These activities give rise to man-made disaster situations, requiring a rapid response. Airpower provides capability to respond with speed. Besides offensive application, airpower provides assistance to military and paramilitary forces, Special Forces (SF) and other state-controlled armed units. Transportation is the first role for rapid induction followed by sustenance. It can provide further assistance in terms of building up Situational Awareness (SA), Intelligence, Surveillance, and Reconnaissance (ISR), setting up an aerial command post and causality evacuation if required. All the roles and activities carried out by the Air Force during peace time under the purview of humanitarian aid and disaster relief and aid to civil authorities, and other agencies, can be utilised in the grey zone warfare. Another aspect related to the land domain grey zone activities is the protection of airpower assets from terrorist attacks (like attack on Pathankot airfield).

**Maritime Domain**. Maritime domain can also be used in the grey zone conflict. Piracy, hijacking, sea borne attack by non-state actors on coastal targets or attacks on oil rigs etc. could be classified under maritime domain grey zone activities. Land domain disaster situations and response would also be applicable in the maritime domain. In addition, disaster situations like oil slick management, sea platform firefighting, maritime rescue and evacuation etc. could also be encountered. Air power instruments can be effectively utilised in assuaging these situations.

**Aerial Domain**. Latest challenge faced by the world, due to grey zone operations in the aerial domain is the sub-conventional threat posed by aerial platforms like, unmanned platforms, drones, swarms, hang gliders and powered gliders etc. These platforms besides being used for direct targeting are also being utilised in roles like ISR, smuggling and arms trafficking etc. In the last few years world over, concerted efforts are being made to deal with these threats. These threats need to be dealt in terms of development and employment of detection systems, anti-drone weapons/systems, engagement procedures and licensing and controlling regulations. Airpower operators, assets and systems are essential component in the entire response for mitigation of these threats.

**Space and Grey Zone**. Space based applications are being utilised in a number of fields like, communications, education, healthcare, navigation and ISR etc., to name a few. Increased reliance on these space-based systems also gives rise to certain vulnerabilities that have a potential for grey zone exploitation. Space operations are suited for grey zone use due to characteristics of ambiguity and difficulty in damage assessment. Anti-satellite warfare includes kinetic weapons like missiles and non-kinetic systems including jammers, laser dazzlers or spoofing equipment. Denial of these systems would have a direct bearing on air warfare especially in terms of navigation, targeting and networked operations.

**Cyber Domain**. This is the most active domain even in peace time. It has the maximum potential for grey zone operations. Cyber domain has become a battlefield with cyber warfare becoming a significant component of present and future conventional and grey zone conflicts. Unlike physical attack, a cyber-attack can be launched instantaneously from anywhere, anytime with little evidence, it is hard to trace and has a high level of deniability. These characteristics make it an ideal and most favoured tool for grey zone operations. Cyber-attacks could be launched against vital infrastructure like banking, power sector and water resource management etc., or military systems and networks. Air power operations are essentially networked operations with platforms, weapons and systems networked in three dimensions (land network, aerial network and network linking ground and airborne systems). Moreover, these networks are further integrated with sister services and other agencies involved with national security apparatus and response. Denial of these networks could prove to be catastrophic and these need to be protected adequately.

**Information Domain**. The prevailing digital age consists of internet, social media apps, and portable electronic devices. The flow of information (or misinformation) is very rapid and its availability is widespread. The narratives can be created, fabricated, changed, or manipulated, and circulated very quickly. This is ideal and advantageous for the grey zone conflict operatives. Post-strike media scrutiny and dissection of Balakot strikes is a classic example, emphasising the importance of not only execution but also need to control the narrative. Airpower practitioners need to have a multi-discipline, multi-domain, institutionalised structure to address these concerns.

## Airpower Utilisation in Grey Zone Conflict

Grey zone conflicts need a whole of government, multi-dimensional approach with the application of all relevant instruments of power at their disposal. Air power resources are an effective military tool for statecraft, characterised by flexibility, lethality, reach, rapid response and creation of shock and awe by effect-based operations. Airpower offers the war fighting components resources that can cover great distances and gain desired lethal and nonlethal effects with great precision. Air power is dynamic in its application and its effects can be switched on or off at ease and it can play an important role in grey zone operational environment. In offensive role it can provide many options, however, its utilisation is not restricted only to offensive role. Airpower can reinforce the nation's course of action against grey zone warfare, with involvement in several direct and supporting roles.

**Offensive Application**. Kinetic application of airpower in the form of aerial attacks is one of the options available to the decision makers. Generally offensive use of airpower on own soil is avoided as it causes further alienation of own people. Multiple options are available even for the aerial attack if so decided. These could be from fighter aircraft, helicopters, or unmanned platforms with a variety of weapons. In grey zone situation generally, precision weapons are preferred to avoid collateral damage.

**Aerial Mobility**. Grey zone situations usually necessitate rapid response making air mobility the preferred option. Airpower can place the ground force into the region where needed and when needed, while also sustaining a critical lifeline into and out of the deployment zone. SF, disaster management teams, their equipment and relief material can be inducted speedily through the medium of air. Both fixed wing transport aircraft and helicopters of varying capability are required for these tasks. Situation may demand large scale expeditionary response or insertion of smaller rapid action teams.

**Situational Awareness**. High degree of situational environment is required in grey zone situations and SA is generally the first victim. It is further corrupted by psychological and propaganda warfare on all pervasive social media. Versatile and adaptable airborne ISR resources are essential to any hybrid campaign. Aerial recce platforms are useful in building the SA through visual, photo and electronic reconnaissance, both by day and night. They have been utilised many a time to ascertain location of trouble spots, disruption or blockades of railway lines and roads and breaches in canal etc. If required aerial command posts can also be established for coordination of the operations.

**Casualty Evacuation**. Occasions do arise when injured personnel needing immediate medical attention may be required to be shifted to places where such facilities are available. These may be during the day or night. Depending on the place of evacuation and numbers of people to be evacuated either fixed wing aircraft in ambulance role or helicopters or combination of both may be required.

**Air Defence (AD)**. AD is a role or task of the Air Force, which is carried out 24x7 not only during war but even during peace time. With the proliferation of unmanned and other smaller platforms the sub-conventional threats, have been added to the list of AD threats. The vital areas and vital installations need to be protected against these threats. The spectrum of AD threats and operations has increased in the grey zone operations scenario. Appropriate detection systems and weapons like Close in Weapon Systems (CIWS) would be required to deal with them.

**Deterrence, Posturing and Strategic Coercion**. These roles and tasks are performed by the airpower instruments in both war and peace situations. They have a large scope even in the grey zone conflict scenarios. The appropriate deployment of assets and flying of specific types of missions can be used for posturing and signalling of intent.

**Defence Diplomacy**. Defence diplomacy is conducted by means of defence cooperation, exchange of visits and joint exercises. Like war and hostile situations, they have a role in the grey zone conflict situations as well.

## Capability Enhancement/Reorientation

Airpower is commonly associated with air-delivered firepower and expeditionary capability. Airpower has a major and decisive role, even in these grey zone situations, and now the air forces world over are equipping and optimising for low-intensity grey zone conflict scenarios. Existing airpower resources offer a large number of options; however, there is a need for some amount of recalibration and reorientation. Certain areas also need capability enhancement. These areas could include capabilities to impose measured costs on adversaries, kinetic and non-kinetic capabilities, lethal and nonlethal weapons, assets protection, organisational adaptations, technology infusion and doctrinal changes.

- **Air Mobility and Logistics Management**. Rapid mobility and induction is vital in grey zone operational scenario. An all-round capability (i.e., heavy and medium lift, fixed wing and rotary wing, manned and unmanned delivery platforms, landed and air dropped) is required. A hub and spoke system of induction and subsequent sustenance works well. Helicopters play and important role in speedy delivery in area of poor connectivity. Large numbers of operating surfaces (helipads and heliports) are beneficial especially in high terrain friction areas. Civil aviation assets with appropriate modifications need to be integrated in this effort. Integrated logistics management systems are equally essential. Automated logistics handling and disbursement ports would enhance the capability further.

- **Surgical Offensive Capability**. Offensive application of airpower invariably will be surgical in nature i.e., with precision avoiding collateral damage. Smart weapons with high degree of accuracy and adequate standoff are highly desirable. Stand-off and precision capability enhancement is a continuous process and more the standoff, better it is. Variety in type and extent of warheads provide more options in terms of effect generated. Air delivered, non-lethal, weapons are also needed in the inventory, as certain situations would require their use. Delivery platforms are also important. Unmanned combat aerial vehicle capability is useful in quite a few situations. Real time intelligence would be essential for kinetic force application.

- **SA Enhancement**. Aerial reconnaissance and surveillance are the best way of obtaining the correct and current picture of the developing situation. Better SA can be obtained by keeping greater area under multiple sensor surveillance with better resolution. Intelligence and surveillance capability need to be enhanced across the spectrum starting from human intelligence to space based surveillance. Aerial vehicles, surface movements, maritime domain, communications and electronic signals need monitoring and all inputs amalgamated to produce a comprehensive battle space picture. Artificial intelligence needs to be embedded in the analysis systems to provide the desired end product on need-to-know basis, with decision support systems and 'What-if' options. Real time monitoring may be required to take on dynamic targets of opportunity. A Joint Surveillance and Target Attack Radar System is highly critical to the success of operations in hybrid warfare.

- **Protection and Security**. The Airpower assets could themselves be targeted in the grey zone warfare. These vital and costly assets would need security and protection from conventional aerial vectors, sub-conventional aerial threats and ground attacks. Multi layered security systems would be required for both aerial and ground threats. The aerial threat mitigation would need systems like CIWS on one end of spectrum to Ballistic Missile Defence (BMD) on the other end. Multiple threat handling systems like S-400 would be ideal for protection of cluster of vulnerable areas/vulnerable points. Automated, networked, technology based security systems would be required for the ground security.

- **All Weather Day and Night Capability**. There is no differentiation between day and night for grey zone activities. Ability to launch and use airpower assets in all types of weather and during day or night is essential. Night vision devices can prove to be a force multiplier in this respect. Portable lighting systems can be of immense use especially in helicopter operations.

- **Special Operation Platforms**. Aerial platforms like C-130 have a lot of utility in grey Zone conflicts. They can be employed in a variety of roles, ranging from logistical transportation to operational tasks like SF team insertions and extraction, airborne command post, aerial cover, firefighting and medical evacuation etc. Their ability to operate from short and unprepared surfaces, adds to their versatility. Roll-on-roll-off kits are available for some of the roles mentioned above and can prove to be economical and practical.

- **Networking and Cyber Domain**. Air operations are highly network centric. In grey zone operations flow of information to numerous stake holders is especially important. Integrated networks with good architecture, supported by suitable applications will assist in building situational awareness, planning, communicating, and monitoring of situation in real time. The information flow would have to be needed to know basis to avoid paralysis due to information overload. The networks would have to have redundancies and protection measures in terms of firewalls and anti-virus systems. Monitoring control rooms with Quick Reaction Teams would help in ensuring their continued availability during hostile activity.

- **Space Based Capabilities**. The term airpower has changed to aerospace power with the aerial warfare envelope expanding to the domain of space. Space based systems and applications are embedded in every aspect of aerial warfare. In Grey zone warfare the involvement of space-based equipment and systems is on an even larger scale. From airpower operations point of view the most important capability enhancement required is in the space-based surveillance capability. Enhancement is required in terms of revisit and resolution, converting reconnaissance capability into surveillance capability.

- **Psychological War and Media**. Psychological warfare or perception war is a vital component of Grey Zone operations and is deeply embedded in them. Media engagement plan and organisational structure needs to be in place for perception management and narrative control. All stake holders need to work collectively in sync with each other. Appropriately equipped and manned operations room working round the clock is necessary for monitoring and conducting these operations.

- **Organisational Adaptation**. Organisational adaptation is required for managing the grey zone conflicts and operations. Appropriate organisational structures need to be created to investigate aspects related to information warfare, electronic warfare, cyber and space operations, strategic and SF operations and technology fusion. Intention would be to develop a multi-domain rapid reaction mechanism. A proactive approach will be even better. A multi-discipline body like an aggressor group could be formed with a charter to monitor the environment, play devil's advocate by identifying possible threats and generating possible grey zone scenarios.

## Conclusion

The world at large and India in particular will be in grey zone conflict scenario for a long time. Airpower has a major role in these grey zone operations. There is a need to be prepared to tackle unpredictability and not get surprised. This requires a change in mind-set and some amount of reorientation and training. In grey zone operations anything can be turned into and used as a weapon therefore, all the contingencies cannot be predicted.

The need of the hour is to develop a high degree of resilience, so as to adapt to changing situations rapidly. Finally, innovation and out of the box thinking is essential.

## End Notes

[1] Synergy, Journal of the Centre for Joint Warfare Studies, Feb 2020.

[2] Aerospace and grey zone warfare, Air Mshl Anil Chopra, PVSM, AVSM, VM, VSM (Retd)

[3] https://warontherocks.com/2019/04/blurring-the-line-part-iii-airpower-applications-in-the-gray-zone/

[4] https://www.airforcemag.com/article/1009hybrid/

[5] https://cenjows.in/upload_images/pdf/Synergy_Aug_2019_BW.pdf

[6] https://www.japcc.org/countering-hybrid-threats-with-air-power/

[7] https://secure.afa.org/Mitchell/presentations/050109hybrid_slides.pdf

[8] https://www.sldinfo.com/wp-content/uploads/2016/01/Airpower-and-the-Hybrid-Threat.pdf

[9] https://cco.ndu.edu/News/Article/1680696/examining-complex-forms-of-conflict-gray-zone-and-hybrid-challenges/

[10] https://media.defense.gov/2017/Jun/19/2001764908/-1/-1/0/AP_0002_GRAY_AIRPOWER_ADVANTAGE_FUTURE_WARFARE.PDF

[11] https://www.bournemouth.ac.uk/news/2019-06-17/explainer-what-hybrid-warfare-what-meant-grey-zone

[12] https://www.airforcemag.com/gray-zone-conflict-drives-space-weapons-development/

[13] https://defense.info/re-shaping-defense-security/2020/11/raaf-prepares-for-gray-zone-operations/

[14] https://cenjows.in/upload_images/pdf/Synergy_Aug_2019_BW.pdf

# 11

# Maritime Grey Zone Operations: Lessons, Implications and Options

**Captain Sarabjeet S Parmar (Retd)**

**Abstract**

*Over the years the term Grey Zone operations has been added to the lexicon of diplomats, the military, and analysts. By and large, the definition places the execution of such operations between peace and stops short of conflict, seeking to achieve strategic objectives without inciting conflict. Such operations have therefore extended the traditional envelope of diplomatic and military engagements by leveraging deployment of traditional military arms, paramilitary forces, and even civilians by exploiting aspects of lawfare weaved through differing interpretations of international laws. The maritime domain has witnessed extensive grey zone operations, which continue to grow, as affected nations are still searching for a resolute addressal mechanism short of conflict. This article will examine the nuances of China's Grey Zone operations in the maritime domain and analyse the implications while seeking plausible options short of conflict.*

## Introduction

The Atlantic Council places the grey zone as a space 'In which defensive and offensive activity occurs above the level of cooperation and below the threshold of armed conflict'. In this space, the council links grey zone operations, activities, and actions to clandestine, covert, unofficial, or outside accepted norms of behaviour, a part of hybrid warfare, as well as activities that 'Can occur during active armed conflict between actors'.[1] It is evident that grey zone operations have a far-reaching impact on stability and security by complicating evolution of an effective addressal methodology. This is more acute in an environment like the maritime domain where nations and their maritime forces are expected to operate in accordance with international laws and conventions, while respecting customary law, especially in areas beyond the territorial seas. While some nations, like the United States (US) in its 2022 National Defence Strategy, have placed emphasis on addressing such operations; the overall lack of capacity and capability to address these operations has left a doctrinal gap that needs to be filled in quickly. While there are operational strategies evolving, they at best address situations as they develop. Nations like China are taking advantage of this gap and based on their respective interpretations of international laws and conventions carry out grey zone operations to further their respective national interests, while maintaining the level below the scope of a hard military response. While there is no time, and tested addressal methodology the Rand Corporation has outlined a four-part framework for responding to grey zone threats.[2] This article will analyse China's grey zone operations and the implications and lessons for India while examining plausible options short of conflict.

## Genesis, Evolution, and Ongoing Praxis

Over contemporary times the line between conflict and peace has blurred to such an extent that it was necessary to view it as a grey area. The second edition of Dieter Flecks edited book published in 2008 on International Humanitarian Law stated that "The line between participation in an armed conflict and neutrality is no longer as clear as it once was. Between the two there is now a grey area in which a state engages in non-neutral service without overtly becoming a party to the conflict".[3] A study of warfare over the centuries and a study of ancient scriptures could indicate that grey zone operations were also conducted when there was a clearer distinction between war and peace. For example, the translation of *Arthashastra* (Economics) by Dr R Shamasastry indicates the possibility of such operations. "Or if a King thinks: That by keeping the peace I can undertake productive works of considerable importance and destroy at the same time those of my enemy... or I can destroy the works of my enemy by employing spies and other means...".[4] Julian Corbett in his treatise on England in the seven years' war (1756-1763) covers how England and France conducted sub-kinetic maritime conflict and engaged in diplomatic campaigns to win allies and partly controlled proxy wars that involved native American allies. This involved the use of both regular and irregular forces.[5]

A more contemporary definition of grey zone challenges was stated in the 2015 US Special Operations Command White Paper 'The Grey Zone' as, "Competitive interactions among and within state and non-state actors that fall between the traditional war and peace duality".[6] China's approach to grey zone operations is under the rubric of military operations other than war. The Science of Military Strategy 2020 edition published by China's National Defence University defines non-war military operations as "Carried out by a country or political group to achieve a certain political goal, using military force, using non-violent or limited violent means".[7] The book further states that such operations are "Dynamic and developing"[8] and while the guidance for non-war military operations and war "Are the same in main aspects",[9] the former "Have some characteristics and laws that are different from war".[10] The book also states that "Non-war military operations are a comprehensive contest conducted by combining military forces with political, economic, and diplomatic struggles in various fields. Without the active cooperation of other means, it is difficult to achieve political goals by military means alone".[11]

This approach is amplified by the manner China operates, in pursuit of political aims, interprets international laws and conventions like the United Nations (UN) Convention on the Law of the Sea (UNCLOS), and aggressively pushes the envelope of confrontation while stopping short of conflict. It is highly unlikely that China will fire the first shot but would avail of an opportunity to claim actions based on self-defence under the UN Charter. The deployment and actions of China in the South China Sea (SCS), and stances at dialogues and discussions conducted at global and regional platforms, are a clear indication of how China uses the combination of military power, economics, and diplomacy as a powerful tool for conducting maritime grey zone operations. This is in conformity with China's 'Three Warfares' approach. Therefore, China's approach to grey zone operations will use all instruments of national power. A 2022 Rand research report pointed out that over the past decade China had employed nearly 80 different grey zone tactics across all instruments of power against Taiwan, Japan, Vietnam, India, and the Philippines. However, due to the economic and military strengths of Japana

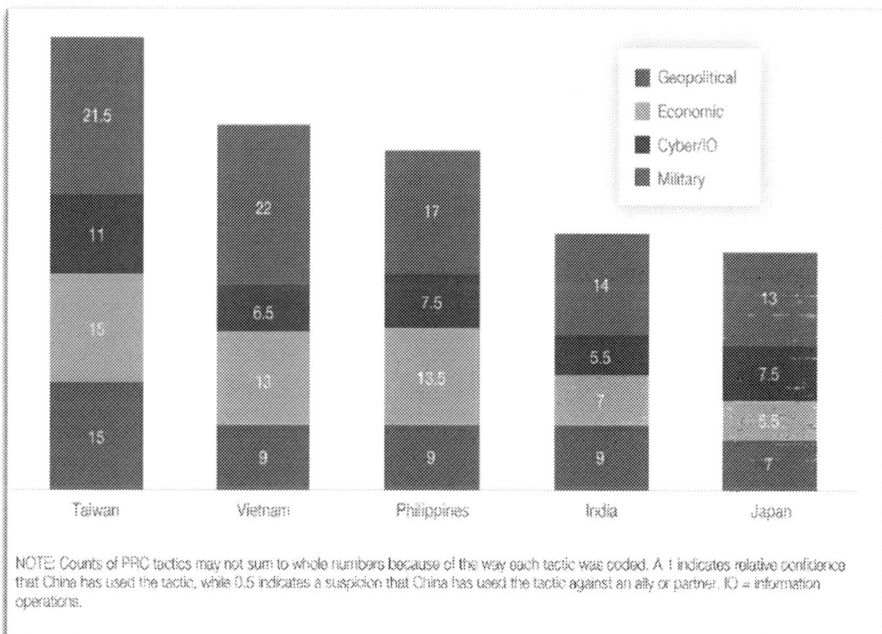


**Figure 1: China's Use of Four Elements of National Power in Grey Zone Operation**

*Source:* *Rand Research Report on Compeition in the Grey Zone: Countering China's Coercion against US Allies and Partners in the Indo-Pacific*

and India, China employs a smaller set of tactics against these two nations as compared to the other three nations.[12] Figure 1 depicts the four elements of national power used by China in the conduct of grey zone operations against these five nations.[13] The report also brought out that China had introduced the term for grey zone (灰色地带) to the Chinese literature following their analysis of recent Western (particularly US) and Japanese literature.[14]

The report also mentioned US grey zone operations conducted since 1945 as identified by China (see Figure 2).[15] Therefore, it is obvious that nations who have powerful instruments of national power will bring to bear on adversarial nations grey zone operations, as these operations can deliver significant cost-effective advantages at a fraction of the cost of conflict to achieve the same aims. The present arrangement of alliances and strategic partnerships provides the umbrella wherein for greater common aims and objectives nations willingly overlook certain actions. For example, in the US-India case, the US has been conducting Freedom of Navigation Operations (FONOPS) against India, of which, the maximum number are conducted against India's stance regarding the need of notification for the innocent passage of warships in India's territorial sea and the conduct of military activities in its Exclusive Economic Zone (EEZ) without seeking India's consent. While FONOPS are still conducted by the US, these actions are overlooked by India given the larger benefits that both the nations enjoy from their comprehensive global strategic partnership. There has been a spurt of activities against Taiwan perhaps due to the lessons being learnt from the Russia-Ukraine war, and the Philippines due to its response against Chinese activities in its EEZ. Hence, this section briefly looks at Chinese grey zone operations in the maritime domain against these two nations and India.

**Against China**

- US military alliances in the Indo-Pacific and activities to strengthen alliances
- US deployment, posture, and presence in the Indo-Pacific, including presence operations, military training, military exercises, and surveillance and reconnaissance operations
- Strategic ambiguity toward Taiwan
- Secret support to Chinese Tibetan separatists
- Sending US Navy research vessels to Taiwan
- Use of think tanks and media to propagate anti-Chinese information
- Labelling China a revisionist country

**Against other Countries**

- Security competition with the Soviet Union during the Cold War
- Covert operations to penetrate and undermine communist countries in Eastern Europe during the Cold War
- Plans to assassinate Cuban leader Fidel Castro
- Efforts to undermine the Salvador Allende government in Chile

**SCS-specific Activities**

- US FONOPs, including those conducted with allies
- B-52 bomber flights over the SCS
- Surveillance and reconnaissance operations
- The Southeast Asia Maritime Security Initiative, intended to increase the maritime capabilities of the Association of Southeast Asian Nations (ASEAN) countries
- Involvement of the US Coast Guard in SCS activities
- Support for the Philippines' UN arbitration case against China concerning the SCS
- Disinviting China from the Rim of the Pacific exercise
- Blaming China for militarizing the SCS
- Shaping the narrative by connecting economic issues, such as trade and investment, with maritime security

**Figure 2: Examples of PRC Identification of US Grey Zone Activities**

*Source: Rand Research Report on Compeition in the Gray Zone: Countering China's Coercion against US Allies and Partners in the Indo-Pacific*

## India

China via the instruments of diplomacy and economic power sought to seek an entry into the Indian Ocean region (IOR) through the Belt and Road Initiative (BRI) targeting India's immediate neighbours, and island nations and other IOR nations friendly with India. Out of the immediate neighbours and island nations, Pakistan, and more recently Maldives, pose a major challenge for India. The main aim has been to reduce Indian influence in the IOR while increasing China's. Thus, the BRI lies at the heart of China's maritime grey zone operations in the Indian Ocean. Over a period of time China's assertive behaviour in the IOR is intensifying, raising the challenges and impacting geopolitical stability in the region. Piracy and the present instability caused due to attacks by the Houthis on shipping in the Red Sea provides China with the opportunity to position warships in the region. While Freedom of Navigation (FoN) is an internationally acceptable practice, one blatant example of positioning of assets 'Not equal to the task' is the deployment of Chinese submarines on anti-piracy patrols in off the Coast of Somalia. While most of the ports that China has invested in like Hambantota, Maldives, Djibouti and Karachi, the port of Karachi would remain a strong point for China in times of conflict as the laws of neutrality could render the other ports unavailable for operations. India has been taking actions, to strengthen its position as a maritime power, and being termed as a preferred security partner and first responder, through the triad approach of diplomatic and maritime engagements and exercises, maritime military modernisation, and developing strategic partnerships. India's support to Sri Lanka in the wake of its debt burden to China is an example India's approach to ensure stability in the region. While China's deployment of its coast guard and maritime militia coupled with strong armed assertiveness has so far been confined to the SCS it is possible that in time these deployments and actions could also be exported to the IOR. While most of the ships and fishing vessels have stayed out of India's

EEZ there have been instances of incursions. In a 2019 incursion, a Chinese research vessel was intercepted by the Indian Navy near Port Blair and was asked to leave Indian waters.[16] There has been an increase in the presence of such research vessels, especially when India conducts missile firing tests and these are only going to increase as India develops more indigenous missiles. While Sri Lanka has put a year long moratorium on the entry of research ships into its ports, an act that is synchronous with India's security concerns, these ships are now entering Maldives.[17] Therefore, there is a need for India and its Navy and Coast Guard to develop a doctrinal approach and strategy to counter such presence and actions.

## Taiwan

China's efforts for the reunification of Taiwan have seen an escalation of tensions due to the myriad of actions taken by her, especially across the Taiwan Strait. The maritime grey zone operations directed towards Taiwan pose a significant threat to its sovereignty and regional stability. The intensity of such operations has increased since the Russia-Ukraine conflict started and seems to stem from what China sees as the response from the US and its allies, which stopped short of an active involvement. It is possible that China sees a similar response in the case of Taiwan even though there is an alliance with the US. On the side-lines of the 30th Asia-Pacific Economic Cooperation Summit meeting in Nov 2023, Xi Jinping told Joe Biden that the reunification of Taiwan will take place peacefully and not by force, though the timing has not yet been decided.[18] However, the actions by China raises questions on the peaceful reunification script. One of the primary tactics employed by China is the use of non-military vessels like fishing boats and coast guard ships to assert control over disputed wasters. These vessels operate in close proximity to Taiwan's maritime zones. Chinese fishing fleets frequently enter the waters claimed by Taiwan, thereby exacerbating disputes while increasing the risk of confrontation. These operations pose challenges to Taiwan's military forces, especially maritime forces that are tasked to enforce Taiwan's sovereignty and sovereign rights provided for by UNCLOS.

In addition to the employment of civilian vessels, China has been deploying military ships and aircraft thereby increasing its military presence. These are provocative actions that can be assumed to test Taiwanese military resolve and capability and also the response acumen of the US and its allies. Air Defence Identification Zone (ADIZ) incursions by China has added to the list of grey zone operations. Since Sep 2022, Taiwan's Ministry of

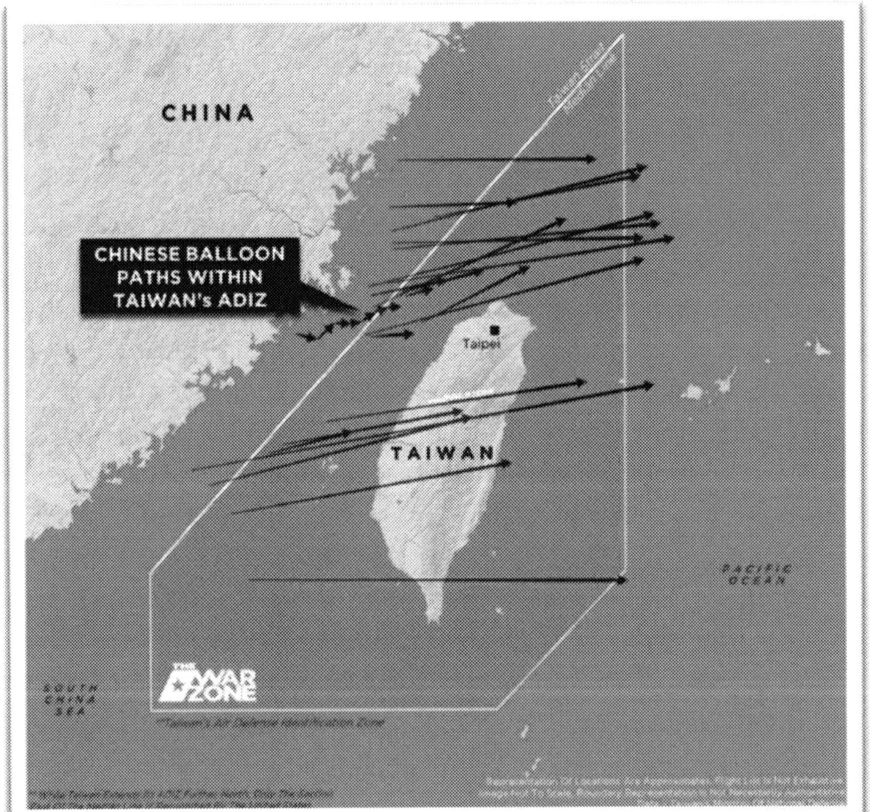


**Figure 3: Chinese Balloon Incursions Dec 2023 to Jan 2024**

*Source: Spike in Chinese Ballons over Taiwan a Serious Threat, The War Zone*

National Defence (MND) started releasing reports on ADIZ incursions by Chinese military aircraft.[19] Chinese warships carry out maritime patrols and transits in the Taiwan Strait though there have been no acknowledged cases of the ships crossing the Taiwan Strait centre line, also called the median line.[20] The line was created during the Cold War and while Taiwan's MND provided the coordinates in 2019, there is no official agreement that supports acceptability by China. Recently, China while defending ongoing exercises has denied the existence of the median line and saturated maritime areas around Taiwan with balloons, drones and civilian boats.[21] Balloons are a new low-cost entrant in grey zone operations that can raise the threat level exponentially, as they can be used for intelligence gathering while posing a flight safety risk to civil aviation. In early 2023, China had flown high altitude balloons through US and Canadian airspace, and four were shot down.[22] Figure 3 shows the median line, Taiwan's ADIZ and incursions of Chinese balloons in the ADIZ from Dec 2023 to Jan 2024.[23]

Taiwan's response to deter Chinese continued aggression has included upgradation of military hardware, like acquisition of advanced naval assets and missile defence systems. It also seeks to continuously enhance cooperation with its allies, particularly the US.

### The Philippines

Scarborough Shoals, which are located in the EEZ of the Philippines, are one of the most contentious areas of dispute between China and the Philippines. In 2012, China seized control of the Scarborough Shoal from the Philippines and positioned large numbers of government and fishing vessels in the vicinity of the shoal, which outnumbered the numbers of Philippines ships. Despite the 2016 international arbitration ruling, Beijing has maintained a continuous presence in the Scarborough Shoal, which supports fishing by Chinese boats while stopping Filipino fishermen from fishing in their own EEZ. China's maritime militia, often disguised as fishing vessels, harass and intimidate Philippine fishermen, further exacerbating tensions in the region.

In addition to the Scarborough Shoal, China has also pursued aggressive activities around the Spratly Islands, constructing artificial islands equipped with military facilities and asserting control over strategic waterways. These actions not only challenge Philippine sovereignty and sovereign rights but also impacts FoN and undermines the rules-based international order. China has also continuously interfered and stopped ships supported by the Philippine Coast Guard from replenishing the Filipino outpost on the Second Thomas Shoal. Intimidation tactics include the use of water jet canons, ramming and blocking by resorting to close quarter situations.

To counter China's maritime expansionism, the Philippines has strengthened its defence cooperation with traditional allies such as the US and sought support from regional partners through mechanisms like Association of Southeast Asian Nations (ASEAN). The Philippines has also emphasised the importance of upholding international law and the peaceful resolution of disputes through dialogue and multilateral cooperation.

## Lessons, Implications and Options for India

It is evident that China tailors its grey zone operations as per the target nation and thus has many options to exercise. These are amply supported by the growth of China as an economic and military power and are also supported by suitable national laws that have been passed. A 2019 Rand Corporation report identifies four areas for response options: military, diplomatic, informational, and economical.[24] These are centred on the US response capacity and capability and most nations would find the four areas, especially military and economical, beyond their capacity and capabilities. To formulate a cogent response, nations would have to band together and bring to bear the aggregate of their national instruments of power to establish comprehensive and suitable response mechanisms. This would require the setting aside of differences for the attainment of major common goals. This is more applicable in the SCS where all the disputant nations have clashing claims, for island features and maritime zones. There is convergence on the interpretation of certain UNCLOS issues by many nations of South and Southeast Asia, including China, especially on the aspects of notification or approval for the innocent passage of warships in territorial seas and approval of the coastal nation for the conduct of military activities in its EEZ. While these interpretations can be enforced against China in the IOR, the disputed waters of the SCS offer the option of nations acting in consonance against China using the same approach China does. For example, Vietnam and the Philippines, which are facing the brunt of China's grey zone operations could work together, duly supported by India. These factors position India in the right place to address China's grey zone operations in the IOR, in line with international law, and rules of engagement, while protecting national and regional interests. Further, for India there exist multiple options which can be exercised based on the advantage accrued by its geographical position and continuous growth as a maritime nation with a strong economy.

India can exercise two distinct options. First would be an IOR focussed approach, where India can bring to bear both maritime deployments, and diplomatic and economic support options. While support to Sri Lanka falls in the latter category, mission-based deployments of the Indian Navy and diplomatic manoeuvring fall in the first category. The success of Operation Sankalp[25] to combat the spurt in piracy and attacks on merchant shipping in the Red Sea adds to the growing recognition of India as a 'Preferred Security Partner' and 'First Responder'. This will aid India in addressing the presence of China, especially its research vessels in areas adjacent to its maritime zones. The recent deployment of 11 submarines, along with the deployed surface and air assets[26], adds to the deterrent value and signals India's intent to closely monitor Chinese presence and movements. The second option for India could involve enhancing its global strategic partnerships and security cooperation with other countries beyond the IOR to counter China's presence and influence in other regions. This could include strengthening partnerships in the Indo-Pacific, participation in multilateral security fora, defence cooperation with strategic partners: including the US, Japan, Australia, and key European countries, strengthening regional security architecture and leveraging its economic and infrastructure initiatives, such as the International North-South Transport Corridor and the Asia-Africa Growth Corridor to expand its influence and connectivity in regions of strategic importance.

In areas beyond the IOR, especially the SCS, support for friendly nations would be via strongly worded statements similar to Chinese statements, as was done recently for the Philippines, stressing on the issue of sovereignty which is the base for disagreements in the SCS.[27] Sovereignty is a sensitive issue for China as after the tribunal judgement in the case of Philippines and China, which favoured the Philippines. China has been pursuing the path of sovereignty over islands in the region through the Four Sha Claim approach.[28] An increase in mission based deployments in the SCS to enhance interoperability via institutionalised exercises would increase the legitimate presence of India's maritime forces. The exercise with ASEAN navies, the inaugural ASEAN India Maritime Exercise held in May 2023, culiminating in the SCS has expanded the ambit by adding to the number of bilateral exercises established earlier. A balanced presence of both Indian grey and white hulls has been brought about by the recent visit of an Indian Coast Guard Ship to the Philippines, Vietnam, and Brunei, which was preceded by visits to Cambodia, Malaysia, Singapore, Thailand, and Indonesia.[29] This balanced presence could follow through a convergent approach on matters maritime in the SCS, especially addressal of non-traditional threats and challenges, in a similar manner that the People's Liberation Army Navy and Chinese Coast Guard follow.

## End Notes

[1] Scowcroft Centre for Strategy and Security Private Workshop, "Scoping the gray zone: Defining terms and policy priorities for engaging competitors below the threshold of conflict", Atlantic Council, December 22, 2022, https://www.atlanticcouncil.org/wp-content/uploads/2022/12/Scoping-the-Gray-Zone_Strategic-Insights-Memo.pdf (Accessed February 13, 2024)

[2] Lyle J Morris et al, "Gaining Advantage in the Gray Zone: Response Options for Coercive Aggression Below the Threshold of Major War", Rand Corporation, 2019, https://www.rand.org/content/dam/rand/pubs/research_reports/RR2900/RR2942/RAND_RR2942.pdf (Accessed February 13, 2024)

[3] Dieter Fleck (ed), "The Handbook on International Humanitarian Law", Second Editon, Oxford University Press, New Yok, 2008, p 58

[4] Dr R Shamasastry, "Kautilyas Arthasastra", Low Price Publications, New Delhi, 2012, p 294

[5] For more details see Geoffrey Till, "Grey Zone Operations: The Rules of the Game", IDSS Paper, RSIS Publication, April 05, 2022, https://www.rsis.edu.sg/rsis-publication/idss/ip22023-grey-zone-operations-the-rules-of-the-game/ (Accessed March 09, 2024)

[6] US Special Operations Command, "The Gray Zone", White Paper, September 09, 2015, p 1, https://specialforcestraining.info/docs/GrayZones-USSOCOM-WhitePaper9Sep2015.pdf (Accessed March 08, 2024)

[7] Xiao Tianliang et al, "The Science of Military Strategy (Revised in 2020)", National Defence University Press. Beijing, January 2020, translated and printed by the China Aerospace Studies Institute, Air University, Montgomery USA, p 289

[8] Ibid. p 290

[9] Ibid. p 290

[10] Ibid

[11] Ibid, p 304

[12] For more details see Bonny Lin et al, "Competition in the Gray Zone: Countering China's Coercion Against U.S. Allies and Partners in the Indo-Pacific", Rand Corporation Research Report, March 30, 2022, https://www.rand.org/pubs/research_reports/RRA594-1.html (Accessed March 09, 2024)

[13] Ibid, p vi

[14] Ibid, p 11

[15] Ibid, p 14

[16] Rajat Pandit, "Indian Warships Chase Away Chinese Vessel Near A&N Islands, Amid Ongoing Shadow-Boxing in IOR," Times of India, December 04, 2019, https://timesofindia.indiatimes.com/india/indian-warships-chase-away-chinese-vessel-near-an-islands-amid-the-ongoing-shadow-boxing-in-ior/articleshow/72353612.cms (Accessed March 09, 2024)

[17] Ritu Sharma, "Sri Lanka Denies Permission To Chinese 'Spy' Vessel to Dock In The Country; Imposes One Year Ban", The Eurasian Times, January 01, 2024, https://www.eurasiantimes.com/sri-lanka-denies-permission-to-chinese-spy-vessels-to-dock/ (Accessed March 09, 2024); and Sachin S Parashar, "Maldives ignores India, lets Chinese spy vessel dock", The Times of India, January 24, 2024, https://timesofindia.indiatimes.com/city/delhi/maldives-allows-chinese-spy-vessel-docking-ignoring-indias-concerns/articleshow/107097044.cms (Accessed March 09, 2024)

[18] Kristen Welker et al, "Xi warned Biden during summit that Beijing will reunify Taiwan with China", *NBC News*, December 20, 2023, https://www.nbcnews.com/news/china/xi-warned-biden-summit-beijing-will-reunify-taiwan-china-rcna130087 (Accessed March 09, 2024)

[19] Ben Lewis, "2022 in ADIZ Violations: China Dials up the Pressure on Taiwan", CSIS, March 23, 2023, https://chinapower.csis.org/analysis/2022-adiz-violations-china-dials-up-pressure-on-taiwan/ (Accessed March 09, 2024)

[20] Bonny Lin, p 57

[21] Mary Anne Sioco, "Chinese Defense Ministry rejects Taiwan Strait median line", Radio Taiwan Intl, March 01, 2024, https://en.rti.org.tw/news/view/id/2010801 (Accessed March 09, 2024); and Yimou Lee, "China steps up grey-zone warfare to exhaust Taiwan, defence report says", Reuters, March 07 2024, https://www.reuters.com/world/china/china-steps-up-grey-zone-warfare-exhaust-taiwan-defence-report-says-2024-03-07/?taid=65e 926b 90586 1200017 14b0c&utm_campaign=trueAnthem:+Trending+Content& utm_medium=trueAnthem&utm_source=twitter (Accessed March 09, 2024)

[22] Stetson Payne, "F-22 Shoots Down another Object, This Time over Canada (Updated)" The War Zone, February 11, 2023, https://www.twz.com/f-22-downs-another-unidentified-object-over-canada (Accessed March 09, 2024)

[23] Thomas Newdick, "Spike in Chinese Ballons over Taiwan a Serious Threat", The War Zone, January 08, 2024, https://www.twz.com/sudden-spike-in-chinese-balloons-over-taiwan-a-serious-threat (Accessed March 09, 2024)

[24] For more details see Lyle J Morris et al

[25] Government of India/ Ministry of Defence Press Release, "Indian Navy's Ongoing Maritime Security Operations ('Op Sankalp') 14 Dec 23 To 23 Mar 24", March 23, 2024, https://pib.gov.in/PressReleaseIframePage.aspx? PRID= 2016201 #:~:text=Today%2C%2023%20Mar%202024%2C%20 marks,in %20the%20Indian%20Ocean%20Region. (Accessed March 28, 2024)

[26] MI News Network. "Indian Navy Deploys 35 Warships & 11 Submarines In The Indian Ocean To Counter Growing Chinese Presence", Marine Insight, March 25, 2024, v (Accessed March 28, 2024)

[27] Express News Service, "South China Sea dispute | India supports Philippines in upholding its sovereignty: Jaishankar in Manila", *Indian Express*, March 27 2024, https://indianexpress.com/article/india/south-china-sea-dispute-india-supports-philippines-in-upholding-its-sovereignty-jaishankar-in-mani la-9235188/#:~:text=Amid%20Manila's%20dispute%20with% 20Beijing, including%20in%20defence%20and%20security (Accessed March 28, 2024)

[28] Julian Ku and Chris Mirasola, "The South China Sea and China's 'Four Sha' Claim: New Legal theory, Same Bad Argument", Lawfare, September 25, 2017, https://www.lawfaremedia.org/article/south-china-sea-and-chinas-four-sha-claim-new-legal-theory-same-bad-argument (Accessed March 28, 2024)

[29] The Print Team, "Indian Coast Guard's pollution control vessel visits Philippines, Vietnam, and Brunei", The Print, March 26, 2024, https://theprint.in/defence/indian-coast-guards-pollution-control-vessel-visits-philippines-vietnam-and-brunei/2015699/ (Accessed March 28. 2024)

# 12

# ChatGPT: An Emerging Digital Disruption

**Brigadier Pawan Bhardwaj, YSM**
**Mr Mohamed Zaid**

**Abstract**

*Open Artificial Intelligence's Generative Pre-trained Transformer (GPT)-4 is the most advanced natural language processing model currently available, with unmatched language finesse and the ability to analyse charts and evaluate its own performance. While there are competitors in the market, none match the prowess yet. China's failed attempts to launch an indigenous version may force it to take special measures to stay relevant. GPT-4 collects personal and technical information, which it may share with third parties for business operations or legal obligations. While Europe and America have data protection laws, India struggles with political and industry pushbacks. Indian startups are advised to venerate these issues and exhibit ethical self-regulation standards. GPT-4 has vast potential for military applications, including data curation, information, and cognitive warfare, simplifying complex issues, and connecting various aspects of human resources, training, and operations. It can perform an important role of identifying propaganda material and fake news. Launch of GPT-4 raises humanitarian and labour concerns. With the ability to generate convincing phishing emails, write polymorphic malware, and provide technical assistance, its potential for use in cyberattacks is significant. It can also be used as an assistive tool for cybersecurity, generating reports and educational materials to improve awareness and identify common misconceptions.*

---

This article was published in the USI Strategic Year Book 2023.

## Introduction

Artificial Intelligence (AI) refers to performing tasks that requires human intelligence, understanding natural language, recognising patterns, making decisions, and solving problems. AI technologies use a combination of machine learning, natural language processing, computer vision, and other techniques to analyse data and generate insights that can help businesses and organisations make better decisions, automate processes, and create new products and services.

One of the most exciting developments is the development of Chat Generative Pre-Trained Transformer (GPT)-4, a Natural Language Processing model, a subfield that deals with the interaction between humans and machines through natural language. GPT-4 is a continuation of the generative pre-trained transformer family of language models, created by OpenAI, one of the leading organisations in the field of AI research. This model is designed to generate human-like responses to text prompts, making interaction with machines more intuitive and natural. Its development has significant implications for a range of industries and will influence all walks of human life. However, as with any other technology, its un-regulatory and irresponsible usage is fraught with risks and ethical concerns.

This article seeks to provide readers with an overview of evolution, appraisal of current state, legal and security implications.

## Evolution of GPT-4

The development of GPT-4 can be traced back to the original GPT model, which was first introduced by OpenAI in 2018. The GPT model was a significant breakthrough in natural language processing, as it was able to generate coherent and realistic responses to text prompts, without the need for explicit supervision. It was based on a transformer architecture, which uses self-attention mechanisms to allow the model to focus on different parts of the input text, depending on the context. The original GPT model was trained on a large corpus of text data, which enabled it to learn the patterns and structures of language and generate responses consistent with the input prompts. The success of the original model led to the development of several versions, finally leading to GPT-4.

GPT-4 is significantly more creative and collaborative, thanks to its increased computational power and the use of more sophisticated techniques. Its neural network architecture consists of an encoder, a decoder, a feed-forward network, and a cross-attention layer.[1] These components generate accurate and contextually relevant human-like text, when it is prompted with and textual or image content. It can generate, edit, and iterate on technical writing tasks, as well as on song and story writing. It accepts images as inputs, analyses them, and responds to a query. With its 25,000 word handling capability it can analyse Uniform Resource Locator query, examine and create long form content creation – useful feature for extended conversations, and analysis.[2] 50 experts from AI safety and cyber security, trained the model's safety features with human feedback, steering it away from disallowed content. It has 100 trillion parameters compared to 175 billion of GPT-3, making it a highly sophisticated language model in the market.

GPT-4 also benefits from a larger (45 gigabytes (GB)[3] of training data, compared to 17 GB for GPT-3) and more diverse training corpus, which includes a wider range of text data sources, widening its comprehension. The responses are more representative of multi-turn conversations, making recommendations, and performing complex calculations. Much like Batman's Alfred Pennyworth, it is ready to do almost anything. It has more language finesse, it understands dialects and slangs, it can create websites based on a picture of a handmade drawing, it can analyse charts[4] of a scientific experiment to summarise results, it can even recommend cooking options[5] when shown picture of ingredients. Exhibiting 'Reflexion', an ability to emulate human-like self-reflection[6] it can evaluate performance, giving it a dynamic memory to enhance its existing reasoning. It can critique its own answers, looks for errors and then rewrite.

## Competitors of GPT-4

**Bing AI by Microsoft**. Bing provides users with more relevant and personalised search results based on their search history, location, and other factors. Called a copilot[7] for the web, it is one. It is a feature of the Bing search engine, utilising GPT technology[8], thus has a training dataset. It brings together search, browsing and chat in one unified experience. It also collaborates with OpenAI's Distributed Automated Language and Learning Entity (DALL-E)[9] (a Generative Adversarial Networks [GAN]) for visual creation capacity, generating images on a textual prompt. The exclusive, standalone, and distinctive feature is its capability is to search the internet[10] for additional and live information, before churning out answers. Accessing resource, rich internet provides Bing with an 'Edge'. Bing AI focuses on leveraging information from multiple search results to respond comprehensively and requires navigating to the Bing search engine, logging into Microsoft account.

**Google's Bard**. Though not supported around the word[11], it is there. Bard is Bidirectional Encoder Representations from Transformers Auto-Regressive Decoder. It is based on Language Model for Dialogue Applications (LaMDA)[12], that provides a range of tools and Application Programming Interfaces (API) for building chatbots and dialogues across a range of input and output channels. It is still experimental, and some of the responses may be inaccurate, so double-check is vital. Experimentation is ongoing and the release is pending. It is unique because it can support audio and voice too.

**Chatsonic**. Invented by Writesonic in 2021, Chatsonic[13] is supported by same technology of ChatGPT. It integrates with Google search, stable diffusion and DALL-E for image generation to create content with the latest information, including visuals and voice commands.[14] It pulls information from Google's Knowledge Graph to create improved and updated answers. It is prone to making factual mistakes, is not very elaborative, cannot generate large amounts of text and needs a subscription plan. Since the free plan is hardly sufficient for viable use and tends to repeat itself, Chatsonic is not fully ready to create codes, yet.

**China**. Though nothing finite exists yet, but China's leadership will not take the Mar AI launch failure of Baidu too well and would ambitiously drive AI technology in a ruthlessly competitive manner than rest of the world to stay relevant in the global AI landscape. Concerns about the potential authoritarian uses will remain, particularly, ethical, data privacy and relentless surveillance:

- **Baidu's Enhanced Representation through Knowledge Integration**. Known as 'Wenxin Yiyan' in Chinese, Baidu failed to release its AI during Mar 2023 highly[15] televised 'Release', plunging[16] the company shares by 10 per cent. It is a Large Language Model (LLM), trained on datasets, scraped from Chinese internet, which itself is already cleaned and purged. It is thus obvious that AI will possess limited utility for non-resident Chinese.

- **Alibaba**. Alibaba's Discovery, Adventure, Momentum, and Outlook Academy, a research institute is under pressure[17] to develop of LLM. In Feb 2023, there was increase[18] in capital from 10 million yuan to 300 million yuan. It also applied for a patent for a 'Human-computer dialogue and pre-trained language model training method, system and electronic equipment.' There is nothing reported in the media or research yet.

## Legal and Privacy Issues

The author prompted ChatGPT to condense the privacy policy[19] of OpenAI which is paraphrased below:

- Personal information will be collected, which includes the user's name, contact information, account details, payment card information, transaction history, personal information in the user chats, and social information from social media pages. Technical information is collected when users use their services, including log data, usage data, device information, and cookies. They utilise analytics and cookies to enhance the user's experience.

- The user's personal information with shared with third parties such as vendors and service providers, for business operations and services, or a transaction without further notice. They may also disclose personal information to comply with legal obligations, protect their rights or property, prevent fraud, or protect personal safety.

GPT-4 could theoretically skim all personal information of the user and threaten privacy infringement. The industry and political pushback[20] forced the withdrawal of India's Personal Data Protection Bill in Aug 2022. While the Indian Government attempts a legal framework to regulate privacy within the digital ecosystem, the unsettled nature of Personally Identifiable Information (PII) will continue to disquiet the users. Illustratively, while the United Kingdom, European Union and European Economic Area protects their data through General Data Protection Regulation[21], the United States (US) dwells on California Consumer Privacy Act.

Indian Information Technology Act, 2000 defines downloading/ copying/extraction of any data[22] from a computer resource (expansively including hardware, network, and database) liable to civil and criminal penalty. Under Section 57 of the 'Indian Copyright Act, 1957', violation may lead to punishment only if the original author Decides' to file a lawsuit[23]. Globally, copyright is taken seriously. Getty Images[24] a stock image giant provided licenses for training AI, 'Respecting personal and intellectual property rights.' It felt belittled when 'Stability AI' allegedly utilised images and committed copyright infringement in 'Pursuit of stand-alone commercial interests'. 'Stability AI' was accused of copying and processing millions of images without obtaining proper licensing. This could be a warning to all the startups in India to be careful and define the limit of innovative talent vs the legality of action, lest it disrupts the cycle of development in India.

## How does GPT-4 Play in Military Arena?

The potential military applications of GPT-4 are vast and varied. The article will analyse and logically map a few cases, potentially for the immediate or near future. The speculative role or uses in the future are deliberately avoided.

- **Curating Data**. Long prompts, image, and graphical analysis, makes GPT-4 a good tool to curate and clean data from different sensors in different file formats, which can be a complex process. Militaries would benefit from this unique capability, supported by the 'Chattiness' of the AI model.

- **Insights from Detailed Reports**. Militaries generate large, iterative, and frequent report formats, which are essential to include wide-ranging aspects of military planning, decision-making and operational processes. GPT-4 will be able to generate easily understandable briefs, citing references, urged on prompt augmentation.

- **Reducing Technology Bias**. Simplification of complex issues, especially technology is a special forte of GPT-4. This will provide a wide variety of support to military analysts and operatives.

❑ **Targeted Training**. High logic and computational capabilities of the language tool can curate focussed training material on the go, simplifying complex issues and connecting various aspects of training and operational areas. It could also assist to generate a wide range of operational scenarios for training, especially those that may be a 'Wild Card' or 'Black Swan' events, difficult to fathom or predict without an AI support.

❑ **Updating Training Material**. A military AI model, trained on a large corpus of military-specific text, training manuals, orders, directives, and special instructions, could generate new training materials or summarise existing ones. In the event of a change in directives or instructions, the LLM could recommend changes to training manuals, which otherwise is a cumbersome process using the traditional book-keeping method.

❑ **Operational and Intelligence Analysis**. Textual and image input understanding capabilities may be utilised to examine variety of inputs to ascertain collaborations and generate likely event possibilities, assisting the militaries in intelligence and operational analysis.

❑ **Historical and Military Record Analysis**. Fine-tuned to military needs and trained on focussed data, LLM can process wide and deep insights, identifying patterns, suggesting triggers and estimates to the students and commanders. This could also assist in creation of 'Decision Support Systems', when supported by 'Battle Space' inputs.

❑ **Digital Staff Officer**. GPT-4 has a wide role capability to perform human resources and administrative role. Assisting in creating reports, updating spreadsheets, and organising files, drafting memos, preparing presentations, and proofreading documents. A cross-functional Deloitte team[25] worked with the Australian military to scope, design, configure, test, and pilot the automated assistants. The team identified and classified all current and anticipated work types, then mapped them according to the level of importance of the work and the cognitive power required to do it. This map provided options about which work could be augmented with AI aka chatbots, supported by LLM, to what extent and in what sequence. Pilot projects built as proofs of concept, freed 10 per cent of the soldiers for higher-value tasks.

- **Translation**. GPT-4 could be used for language translation for the military. This would also assist militaries to read and analyse adversary's primary literary sources too. This is an easier and ready option, compared to a focussed AI model for audio translation.

- **Information and Cognitive Warfare**. GPT-4 has the largest variety of tasks in interdependent fields of technology and psychology.[26] Sentiment analysis from various social media inputs, content creation to affect target population or to motivate friendly population, all is possible with this unique tool. It is 'Intelligent' enough to understand the subtle and unique linguistic and cultural characteristics of users and can be coaxed to generate text that is relevant to a user's cultural background, slangs, idioms, and regional expressions. It can adjust and adapt the communication style to target a specific population. This application can be thus exploited to access personal information of the individuals to learn their behaviour or pattern. A digital version of 'Proof of Life'. Concurrently, it will also be prompted to create tools to identify such propaganda material, fake news or deepfakes too.

## General Security Concerns

**Human Communications**. The Colourful Prompt Tuning like language model's smart prompt in electronic communication are routinely short and overtly positive.[27] These prompts will overtime decrease human generated language production, interpersonal perception, and task performance - it is just easier to select a prompt, rather than drafting a detailed reply. An AI generated text prompt is increasingly being regarded as a good option, bolstered by procrastination and AI overreliance.[28]

**Humanitarian Concerns**. Conversational and language model AI will establish itself as daily-use tool make in workplace, automating substantial parts of many jobs. Higher paying desk jobs that depend on digital communication and decision making will take more heat. It is estimated that majority of the US workforce could feel some effect, and all higher paying jobs will observe major changes in their workplaces.[29] Layoffs and workforce reductions may occur in data processing services, information services and publishing industries and also in low order jobs like trainers, stenographers and personnel assistants[30]. Workers in developing countries unable to exploit the capability or download speeds will also suffer from technology apartheid.

**GPT-4's Exploitation Capabilities and Vulnerabilities**. As a technology advances, the need for robust security measures becomes increasingly important. The areas of concern are the architecture - overall framework and organisation of a system and logic map - flow of data and the interaction between various components of a particular technology. Any weaknesses in architecture and logic map of a particular technology can leave a technology vulnerable to exploitation, making it imperative to thoroughly assess and address potential security concerns. GPT-4 is equally vulnerable to such issues.

**Enhancing Performance through Supervised Learning**. It relies on supervised learning[31] to train and reinforce learning by utilising newer and updated training datasets[32] to reflect changes in language usage and new information. This means continually improved performance. Such a system is highly dependent on large amounts of high-quality data while insufficiently cleaned dataset will affect the output. If the training dataset is not cleaned – it could get things wrong and 'Hallucinate'[33] incorrect facts or become gullible to leading questions by the users.

**LLM with Enhanced Capabilities**. As an AI language model, GPT-4 is also designed to learn from user inputs. User feedbacks to questions like "Was this response better or worse or same?" help improve responses over time. If a user corrects or asks a follow-up question, the prompt is used to refine understanding and generate better responses. The authors tested a related hypothesis, if ChatGPT could identify the origin of a particular text? Surprisingly it could identify and also provided date of generation - from a different chat box/login.

**Advancing Multimodal Understanding and Collaboration**. Many users routinely volunteer information to 'Improve' the output. A gullible user may provide information of the company, its core competency, task at hand and details of client to 'Generate a good quality' operational brief, or a research paper, unknowingly providing 'Espionage material'. Such an information in pre ChatGPT era was designated confidential and could be considered breach of non-disclosure agreements. The organisations will have to navigate maze and reword their non-disclosure agreement scripts.

**Navigating the Complexities of Plagiarism in AI-Generated Content**. The fear of plagiarism is also well founded. It is a two-way street. Does GPT-4 not suffer from it when it generates a content? 'Originality AI' provides the plagiarism check to many products. It also claims to the best content detection tool[34] in the market (96 per cent accuracy against 35 per cent by closest competitor) and attributes it to 'Subscription only business model'. It uses 'A Lot' of computational power too. If the content creator aka ChatGPT is plagiarism free, how does the user ensure his content is too? By ethical use. An informed user could counter check the new content by using quality and top line[35] plagiarism checkers like AI-generated content like - OpenAI's AI Text Classifier, GPTZero, Plagibot, Content at Scale and Writer.com

## Cyber Security Issues

Adversarial attacks are a type of cyber-attack in which an attacker deliberately manipulates input data to mislead a machine learning model. A ChatGPT learning from an adversarial data will naturally generate flawed natural language responses, which are more difficult to detect than other types of attacks.

GPT-4 is trained on publicly available content on the internet. As of yet, there seems no API[36] available for third parties to train it on specific content. When it becomes possible the disinformation, phishing, and other attack vectors will increase in numbers and become much more finely tuned and targeted. Improved and convincing phishing emails, including emails in multiple languages will create more attack surfaces for criminals and improve social engineering attacks.

GPT can impersonate[37] an individual style of a real person, if prompted sufficiently. A convincing email from a person in authority could induce subordinates to undertake malicious activities, unwittingly. Business Email Compromise (BEC) is a type of social engineering attack. The attacker creates a fake email that looks like it is from a trusted source, such as the chief executive officer or a vendor. The email may include a sense of urgency, such as a request for an urgent payment or a need for sensitive data. The recipient of the email, thinking it is legitimate, follows the instructions and shares confidential company data or money. Security software usually detects BEC attacks by identifying patterns. However, a BEC attack powered by GPT-4 can get past security filters.

Maliciously oriented clickbait journalism and omnipresence of social media, challenges the differences between real and fake. Politically driven agendas can be accurately curated to target specific audiences, convincingly.

There have been demonstrations of GPT writing a malware. Could an insufficiently skilled criminal, order such a malware. The tool appears to be convincing but could the criminal in context identify an error in the malware? Unlikely. This means that GPT will be useful to experts only 'By saving time', since the expert can validate the output.

Researchers at Cyber Ark have found that GPT-4 can aid malware development. They could coax it to create a highly elusive and difficult to detect polymorphic malware[38] following text-based interactions. They easily evade security products and make mitigation cumbersome with very little effort or investment by the adversary.

Another argument about criminals attempting more complex tasks. Would an expert criminal choose to create a malware and ratify it on the AI model or order creation and approve it in person? Obvious choice would be former, since trying to identify a bug in externally created malware would be much more taxing, irritatingly slow and arduous.

Criminals could however query some advice to a technical problem, which would assist in the activity. If an attacker is struggling to escalate privileges or find data, the model's answer would be more accurate to the context. These answers might help criminals with better and faster attacks, which would be otherwise beyond their capabilities. This also means many more people could create malware, potentially leading to many more attacks and breaches.

It can be an assistive tool to protect cyber interests too. It generates reports and carries out analysis of cybersecurity threats, turns them into reports and share them more widely, in a conversational language. These models have the potential to improve cyber security education and awareness. By analysing text from a variety of educational resources, ChatGPT can identify common misconceptions and areas of confusion, and then curate focussed educational and training material.

## Conclusion

GPT-4 already has an image understanding capability[39], which is considered impressive, so is its capability to analyse graphical representations in a research report. But it is still falls short of further exploitability; multimodal dialogue response generation[40], moves in to fill the gap. It is a new process to generate or understand visual content in collaboration with a textual context. The researchers attempt to generate a multimodal response (e.g., containing both image and text). If proven, it would empower the content creators, entertainment industry, curate highly focussed educational or motivational multimedia content. Could video also form part of this multimodal dialogue? The possibilities are enormously enriching and ominously frightening.

ChatGPT developer, OpenAI has also launched plugins[41] to grant access to third-party knowledge sources including the web. Though restricted testing level availability, it is an interesting update. Can the plugin authenticate the website and its content? Will it countercheck and reorganise the final output after website visit? There are many questions and an exciting future.

GPT-4's business model[42] is yet another aspect to look for in the future. Its API services enable businesses to access digital resources and data, enabling them to create innovative applications and services that improve the customer experience and increase operational efficiency. Premium subscription plans and selling training datasets, provides advanced features and capabilities to their customers. However, the most intriguing aspect is data monetisation, which is the process of extracting value from collected data by selling it to interested buyers for the purpose of developing new models, technologies, and conducting market research. This capability is humongous, since it is collecting a large amounts of data, including PII, tacit knowledge, and general data.

We would let this AI tool conclude about itself [43]with instructive words, conclusion for future use, buoyant, illustrative, considering the security, legal issues, recommending intelligent use by informed users.

- As ChatGPT continues to evolve and improve, the future of this technology is incredibly exciting. With the ability to generate human-like responses, it has the potential to revolutionise communication and interaction between humans and machines. However, as with any new technology, there are also important security and legal considerations to keep in mind.

- One of the biggest security concerns surrounding ChatGPT is the potential for malicious actors to use the technology for nefarious purposes, such as spreading disinformation or carrying out phishing attacks. To address these concerns, it will be important for developers and users alike to implement robust security measures, such as multi-factor authentication and encryption, to prevent unauthorised access to sensitive information.

- In addition to security concerns, there are also legal implications to consider when it comes to using ChatGPT. For example, as the technology becomes more advanced, there may be questions about who is responsible for the responses generated by the system, and whether or not they can be held liable for any negative outcomes resulting from those responses. It will be important for developers and users to stay informed about the legal landscape surrounding ChatGPT to ensure they are in compliance with all relevant regulations and laws.

❑ The future of ChatGPT is bright, but it is important to approach this technology with caution. As users become more familiar, they should be encouraged to use the technology intelligently and responsibly, with an eye towards minimising risks and maximising potential benefits. Ultimately, by working together to address these challenges, we can unlock the full potential of Chat GPT and usher in a new era of human-machine interaction."

The above text perceptibly lacks in quality, which is actually inextricably linked to the instructions provided to the ChatGPT.

## End Notes

[1] Marcin Fr¹ckiewicz, 'The Science Behind GPT-4: Understanding its Architecture and Training Process, 27 March 2023, https://ts2.space/en/the-science-behind-gpt-4-understanding-its-architecture-and-training-process/, accessed on 23 April 2023.

[2] https://openai.com/product/gpt-4, accessed on 23 April 2023.

[3] Daivi, 'GPT3 vs GPT4-Battle of the Holy Grail of AI Language Models, 13 April 2023, https://www.projectpro.io/article/gpt3-vs-gpt4/816#:~:text =Com par ed%20to%20GPT%2D3's%2017,accurate%20results%20than%20 GPT%2D3., accessed on 23 April 2023.

[4] https://blog.tryamigo.com/use-cases-of-gpt-4/, accessed on 24 April 2023.

[5] 'AI engineer asked ChatGPT for recipes from refrigerator pic. The answers were...', MONEYCONTROL NEWS, 17 March 2023, https:// www.moneycontrol.com/news/trends/visual-chatgpt-gpt-4-ai-openai-language-model-chatbots-twitter-ai-recipes-10266611.html, accessed on 24 April 2023.

[6] Loz Blain, 'GPT-4 becomes 30% more accurate when asked to critique itself', 03 April 2023, https://newatlas.com/technology/gpt-4-reflexion/, and https:// arxiv.org/abs/2303.11366, both accessed on 22 April 2023 and

[7] https://blogs.microsoft.com/blog/2023/02/07/reinventing-search-with-a-new-ai-powered-microsoft-bing-and-edge-your-copilot-for-the-web/, accessed on 24 April 2023.

[8] https://www.lifewire.com/what-is-bing-ai-chatbot-7371141#:~:text=The%20 Bing %20AI%20chatbot%20was,into%20answers %20 using%20 natural% 20language., accessed on 24 April 2023.

[9] Andrew Hutchinson, 'Microsoft Integrates DALL'"E Visual Creation Tools into Edge and Bing', 12 March 2023, https://www.socialmediatoday.com/news/ microsoft-integrates-dalle-visual-creation-tools-into-edge-and-bing/645621 /, accessed on 24 April 2023.

[10] https://www.lifewire.com/what-is-bing-ai-chatbot-7371141#:~:text=The%20B ing %20AI%20chatbot%20was,into%20answers%20using%20natural% 20language., accessed on 24 April 2023.

[11] https://bard.google.com/?hl=en, accessed on 24 April 2023.

[12] https://bard.google.com/faq?hl=en, accessed on 24 April 2023.

[13] https://www.makeuseof.com/best-alternatives-chatgpt/, accessed on 24 April 2023.

[14] https://chatsonic.pro/, accessed on 24 April 2023.

[15] https://newatlas.com/technology/baidu-ernie-bot-ai/, accessed on 24 April 2023.

[16] https://arstechnica.com/information-technology/2023/03/chinese-search-giant-launches-ai-chatbot-with-prerecorded-demo/, accessed on 24 April 2023.

[17] Pandaily, 'Alibaba's DAMO Academy Leaders Take Charge in AI Development', 17 March 2023, https://pandaily.com/alibabas-damo-academy-leaders-take-charge-in-ai-development/, accessed on 24 April 2023.

[18] Seaton Huang, 'Tracking the Race to Develop Generative AI Technologies in China', 16Feburary 2023, https://www.cfr.org/blog/tracking-race-develop-generative-ai-technologies-china, accessed on 24 April 2023.

[19] Updated Privacy Policy on 07 April 2023, https://openai.com/policies/privacy-policy, accessed on 20 April 2023.

[20] https://www.dataguidance.com/notes/india-data-protection-overview#: ~:text=In%20 August%202022%2C%20the%20Government,privacy%20 within %20 the% 20digital%20ecosystem, accessed on 21 April 2023.

[21] https://ico.org.uk/for-organisations/dp-at-the-end-of-the-transition-period/ overview-data-protection-and-the-eu/, accessed on 20 April 2023.

[22] https://cis-india.org/internet-governance/blog/privacy/safeguards-for-electronic-privacy, accessed on 20 April 2023.

[23] https://copyleaks.com/blog/a-brief-look-at-plagiarism-in-india#:~:text=Sect ion %2057%20of%20the%20'Indian,infringement%20as%20a%20crimi nal% 20offense, accessed on 21 April 2023.

[24] https://edition.cnn.com/2023/01/17/tech/getty-images-stability-ai-lawsuit/ index.html, accessed on 22 April 2023

[25] 'AI reports for duty in the Australian military', https://www.deloitte.com/global/ en/services/consulting/perspectives/AI-reports-for-duty-in-the-australian-military.html, accessed on 02 March 2023.

[26] Som Biswas, 'Prospective Role of Chat GPT in the Military: According to ChatGPT', 27 February 2023, https://www.qeios.com/read/8WYYOD, accessed on 22 April 2023.

[27] Melissa De Witte, 'How will ChatGPT change the way we think and work? Stanford scholar examines', 13 February 2023, https://news.stanford.edu/2023/ 02/13/will-chatgpt-change-way-think-work/, accessed on 24 April 2023.

[28] Mihaela Vorvoreanu and Samir Passi, 'Overreliance on AI: Literature review', 2022, https://www.microsoft.com/en-us/research/uploads/prod/2022/06/Aether-Overreliance-on-AI-Review-Final-6.21.22.pdf, accessed on 24 April 2023.

[29] Michael Webb, 'The Impact of Artificial Intelligence on the Labor Market', Stanford University, January 2020, https://www.michaelwebb.co/webb_ai.pdf, accessed on 24 April 2023.

[30] Shamika N Sirimanne, 'How artificial intelligence chatbots could affect jobs', 18 January 2023, https://unctad.org/news/blog-how-artificial-intelligence-chatbots-could-affect-jobs, accessed on 24 April 2023.

[31] ChatGPT: The Future of Conversational AI in the Cyber Security Landscape, 06 April 2023, https://emergingindiagroup.com/2023/04/06/chat-gpt-the-future-of-conversational-ai-in-the-cyber-security-landscape/, accessed on 21 April 2023.

[32] Gagan Anand, 'India: The Revolutionary ChatGPT and Its Legal Policies', 01 March 2023, https://www.mondaq.com/india/privacy-protection/1288150/the-revolutionary-chat-gpt-and-its-legal-policies, accessed on 21 April 2023.

[33] David C and Paul J, 'ChatGPT and large language models: what's the risk?', https://www.ncsc.gov.uk/blog-post/chatgpt-and-large-language-models-whats-the-risk, accessed on 21 April 2023.

[34] https://originality.ai/, accessed on 22 April 2023.

[35] Eray Eliacik, 'Is ChatGPT plagiarism free?- Will ChatGPT change the definition plagiarism?', 30 March 2023, https://dataconomy.com/blog/2023/03/ 28/is-chatgpt-plagiarism-free-turnitin-checker/#:~:text=The%20short% 20answer%20is%20yes,of%20AI%20usage%20and%20plagiarism, accessed on 22 April 2023.

[36] Kate Bevan, 'ChatGPT presents new risks – here are five things you can do to mitigate them', https://www.infosys.com/insights/cyber-security/new-risks.html, accessed on 20 April 2023.

[37] https://www.malwarebytes.com/cybersecurity/basics/chatgpt-ai-security, accessed on 20 April 2023

[38] Alessandro Mascellino, 'ChatGPT Creates Polymorphic Malware', 18 January 2023, https://www.infosecurity-magazine.com/news/chatgpt-creates-polymorphic-malware/, accessed on 22 April 2023.

[39] Chetan, 'Analyzing Images with Chat GPT-4 : A First Look', 17 March 2023, https://aivatapi.com/analyzing-images-with-chat-gpt-4-a-first-look/, accessed on 22 April 2023.

[40] Qingfeng Sun, Yujing Wang etal, 'Multimodal Dialogue Response Generation', 2022, https://aclanthology.org/2022.acl-long.204.pdf, pp 2855, accessed on 22 April 2023.

[41] Kyle Wiggers, 'OpenAI connects ChatGPT to the internet', 23 March 2023, https://techcrunch.com/2023/03/23/openai-connects-chatgpt-to-the-internet/, accessed on 22 April 2023.

[42] Gloria Coles, 'How Does Chat GPT Make Money?', https://www.pcguide.com/apps/how-does-chat-gpt-make-money/, accessed on 22 April 2023.

[43] Generated on 21 April 2023 at https://chat.openai.com/

# 13

# Grey Zone Conflict and Legal Derision

**Wing Commander (Dr) UC Jha (Retd)**

**Abstract**

*The 'Grey Zone' conflict falls between the war and peace on the war-peace continuum. It is characterised by intense political, economic, informational, and military show of force. Grey zone actions are not new. Examples of such tactics include cyber warfare, deception, proxy war, economic pressure, digital propaganda, and drones etc. They may also involve a military show of force or intimidation and unconventional military operations. The ambiguous nature of grey zone activity coupled with a lack of well-defined international law makes it difficult to hold grey zone actors accountable for their misdeeds. The United Nations, the largest international player to facilitate conflict management by states, remains an ineffective organ for conflict de-escalation in grey zone conflicts. There is an urgent need to upgrade international legal frameworks and mechanisms of conflict management that could be employed to address the grey zone conflicts.*

## Introduction

If a state is engaged in an armed conflict, it is said that it is at war. If the state is not in an armed conflict, it is at peace. 'Grey Zone' is the space between war and peace involving coercive actions that do not reach the level of armed conflict. Today there are several grey zone conflicts involving confrontations over territory, sovereignty and economic interests. The operations

This article was published in the USI Journal (Apr-Jun 2021)

launched by Russia against Ukraine in 2014, the Russian interference in the 2016 United States (US) Presidential election,[1] the Chinese interventions in the South China Sea, intrusion in Ladakh, and Pakistan's proxy war in Jammu and Kashmir could be termed grey zone activities. Another example of this kind is the killing of the Islamic Revolutionary Guard Corps Quds Force Chief Qasim Soleimani by a US drone strike in Iraq in Jan 2020. In such situations, the use of military forces falls short of actual war but cannot qualify as peace.

A few states are using non-state actors and unconventional tools to destabilise their adversaries. Russian Army General Gerasimov, without explicitly using the term grey zone, has expressed the view that "A perfectly thriving state can, in a matter of months and even days, be transformed into an arena of fierce armed conflict, become a victim of foreign intervention, and sink into a web of chaos, humanitarian catastrophe, and civil war".[2]

The laws of war or International Humanitarian Law (IHL) regulates relations between states by limiting the use of violence in armed conflicts.[3] IHL applies only to international armed conflict or internal armed conflict; it does not cover internal tensions or disturbances such as isolated acts of violence. International law does not clearly set out acceptable norms in many areas of the grey zone. The main reason is that such conflicts do not reach the level of an armed conflict. Besides discussing the concept of grey zone conflict, this article discusses some relevant legal issues such as the effectiveness of the United Nations (UN) Charter and the means and methods of warfare that may be exploited in a grey zone conflict.

## Defining Grey Zone Conflict

Grey zone has been defined by one author as, "Those covert or illegal activities of non-traditional statecraft that are below the threshold of armed organised violence; including disruption of order, political subversion of government or non-governmental organisations, psychological operations, abuse of legal processes, and financial corruption as part of an integrated design to achieve strategic advantage".[4] The US Special Operations Command uses the following definition of grey zone conflict: "Grey zone challenges are defined as competitive interaction among and within state and non-state actors that fall between the traditional war and peace duality. They are characterised by ambiguity about the nature of the conflict, opacity of the parties involved, or uncertainty about the relevant policy and legal frameworks".[5]

The important characteristics of grey zone conflict are:

- It remains below the threshold that would justify a military response with an aim to avoid major clashes, or attributable violations of international law.
- It unfolds gradually over time rather than involving bold, all-encompassing actions to achieve objectives in one step.
- There is a lack of attributability with an aim to disguise its role at least to some extent by using disinformation or/and cyber-attacks.
- There are extensive legal and political justifications, often grounded in historical claims supported with documentation.
- It stops short of threatening the defender's vital or existential interests.
- It is typically built around non-military tools, as part of the general approach of remaining below key thresholds for response.
- It may use the threat of more violent military actions.
- It puts the defender in situations where strong responses appear non-viable or counterproductive, for strategic and domestic political reasons.[6]

Grey zone warfare has been referred to as irregular warfare, political warfare, asymmetric warfare, and unconventional warfare.[7] Such tactics may include cyber-attacks, deception, sabotage, proxy war, assassinations, espionage, economic pressure, terrorism, and exploitation of gaps and ambiguities in the law. Manipulation of public opinion at home and abroad by using information warfare and disseminating 'Fake News' is an important means of creating confusion and scepticism.[8]

## Grey Zone Conflicts and Hybrid Warfare

Grey zone conflict and hybrid war are two different concepts. The use of the term 'Conflict' for the former and 'War' for the latter is intentional. However, hybrid warfare techniques may be used in a grey zone conflict. In such a conflict, conventional military operations may be used alongside non-conventional tactics, whereas in hybrid warfare, conventional military operations are dominant and non-conventional operations are used as auxiliary tactics. Protracted engagement is one of the dominant characteristics of a grey zone conflict, whereas engagements are of short duration in hybrid warfare.[9] Parties engaged in grey zone conflicts use unconventional hybrid warfare tactics such as political and information warfare, propaganda appealing to transnational actors, equipment and training of non-state actors, state-level economic pressures and unconventional operations by the security forces.

## Grey Zone Conflict and the UN Charter

The UN Charter prohibits aggression. Article 2(4) of the Charter states that, "All members shall refrain in their international relations from the threat or use of force against the territorial integrity or political independence of any state, or in any other manner inconsistent with the purposes of the UN". Unlawful uses of force that violate provisions of Article 2(4) generally require forces engaging in military activities whether traditional armed forces or non-state armed groups. In practice, grey zone conflict measures are designed to avoid being identified as clear violations of the Charter even when they do constitute an unlawful use of force. A number of tactics used in grey zone conflict are not accounted for by the Charter's prohibition on the use of force. For example, economic measures, cyber operations, disinformation, and lawfare traditionally do not violate Charter Article 2(4). In theory, the UN Charter's prohibition on the use of force is sufficient to account for grey zone tactics when they resemble traditional military activities. However, when a state employs cyber capabilities in a grey zone conflict to damage or disable infrastructure, it would not amount to the use of force in violation of Article 2(4). Disinformation and criminal activity generally also fall below the threshold of an armed conflict. In fact, it gives an impression that the 'Principle of non-use of force' under Article 2(4) of the Charter has been made impotent by grey zone conflict.

## Applicability of IHL

Classification of contemporary conflict is based on the post-World War II revision of the Geneva Conventions, which are applicable in international and internal armed conflicts. Assessing the existence of armed conflict is easy when the armed forces of states are engaged in hostilities against each other in an inter-state dispute. However, in the case of grey zone conflict, which cannot be classified as 'War or armed conflict', the applicability of IHL remains ambiguous.

In the past few decades, high-tech advancements have altered the means and methods of warfare. Today, the means of grey zone conflict includes surgical operations, restrained and limited use of kinetic forces special operations or irregular forces, cyber warfare, information warfare, the utilization of autonomous weapons, and other non-violent methods of coercive diplomacy like economic sanctions. The states in a grey zone conflict use a mix of strategic and operational techniques, making any resolution arduous. The beginning and termination of conflict remain uncertain because most of the grey zone conflicts opera-tions are undertaken in highly permeable international borders. Since grey zone is a mix of military and non-military measures; application of IHL in the use of means and methods of conflict becomes difficult.[10]

Today, domestic law, international law and judicial institutions are being exploited to influence the military policies of the government. Lawfare is the strategy of using or misusing law as a substitute for traditional military means. It is becoming a powerful 'Force Multiplier', reminding one of Sun Tzu, who once said, "...to fight and conquer in all your battles is not supreme excellence; supreme excellence consists in breaking the enemy's resistance without fighting".[11] It has become an integral element of any grey zone conflict. As such conflicts become more prevalent, relevance of lawfare intensifies. It provides a means to compel specified behaviour with fewer costs than the use of weapons. Lawfare thrives on legal ambiguity and presents challenges to international peace and security by questioning the validity of existing public international law rules. For instance, Peoples Liberation Army's handbook on international law states that officers should not feel completely bound by international laws that are detrimental to China's national interests but should focus on those international laws beneficial to China while evading those harmful to China's interest.[12] Russia, China and the Palestine Authority have used 'Legal Warfare' as a major component of their strategic doctrine. Lawfare is a good substitute for kinetic warfare; the states need to exploit it for strategic advantages.

### Challenges for India

China and Pakistan, based on their own interests and abilities, have developed different grey zone strategies against India. Pakistan is relying on grey zone tactics using what is described as salami tactics, support to terrorism and cross border infiltrations;

whereas China's actions are incrementally changing the territorial status quo. Both these adversaries are using non-military tools of coercion, such as cyber-attacks, propaganda, terrorism, insurgency and covert operations. Such activities are likely to continue using grey zone strategies in the coming years.

To counter a grey zone conflict requires a full spectrum response involving the state's security as well as the private sector. Countering measures against this method of conflict will require more than traditional military strategy responses and must incorporate more than special operations forces or paramilitary operations. The members of special forces may have to undertake clandestine operations in the grey area between overt military operations and covert operations. These members may also have to adopt certain methods like, 'Perfidy' which may be prohibited under IHL.[13]

Non-Lethal Weapons(NLWs) can also play an important role in countering grey zone tactics. The use of such weapons may also be strategically advantageous since conventional weapons may cause unnecessary, indiscriminate or disproportionate harm. The use of NLWs such as chemical riot agents or incapacitating agents may be an effective way of responding to unconventional grey zone threat that may be operating in the area dominated by civilians.

According to Fitton, counter-responses to grey zone tactics would involve further investment in show of force, disinformation, deterrence and manoeuvring adversaries away from grey zone tactics.[14] Grey zone success depends on patience and an ability to blend together all the instruments of state power. One must remember that even a strongest enemy with well-developed armed forces and technologically advanced weapons has some vulnerability. These vulnerabilities need to be exploited at the right time and by appropriate military and non-military means.

The challenges of today are that state and non-state actors do not respect the norms and rules of the international law. Any use of force or threat to use force that is contrary to Article 2(4) of the UN Charter and that fails to meet the requirement of self-defence under Article 51 remains unlawful.[15] In order to achieve an edge in grey zone conflicts, India must:

- Invest in establishing and upgrading its cyber capabilities, improve the intelligence gathering effort against its potential adversaries.
- Intensify the quality and quantity of attacks on targets located near its border through limited military operations.
- Exploit the use of drone technology and use it as a game changer in grey zone conflicts
- Invest in lawfare and devise a comprehensive strategy for its effective exploitation.
- Use NLWs and consider to avoid disproportionate civilian casualties in operations.

## Conclusion

The ambiguous nature of grey zone activity, coupled with a lack of clearly defined law, makes it difficult to hold grey zone actors accountable and develop acceptable countermeasures. The role of non-military means of achieving political and strategic goals has grown in the last decade; they have exceeded the power of weapons in their effectiveness. Today, the internet and social media are creating entirely new opportunities for the mass manipulation of opinion. The rules of war are changing rapidly. Grey zone conflict is a viable and cheap option when compared to a broad military operation. States engaged in grey zone conflicts will continue to exploit weaknesses in adversaries to increase their own relative gains. The international community must recognise that grey zone conflict poses a real danger to the world peace. It must ensure that grey zone conflict does not operate in a legal vacuum. Since IHL fails grey zone conflict, it needs to be updated.

## End Notes

[1] Facebook now estimates that during and after the American election in 2016 a Russian-linked troll farm called the Internet Research Agency was responsible for at least 120 fake pages and 80,000 posts that were directly received by 29m Americans. Through sharing and liking, the number multiplied to nearly 150million, about two-thirds of the potential electorate. "Waging war with disinformation," *The Economist* (25 January 2018).

[2] Valery Gerasimov Valery, "The Value of Science is in Foresight: New Challenges Demand Rethinking the Forms and Methods of Carrying out Combat Operations," *Military Review*, (January-February 2016), 23-29.

[3] IHL achieves this by: (i) Geneva Conventions of 1949—sparing those who do not or no longer directly participate in hostilities (for example civilians; injured, sick or wounded soldiers; or those who have surrendered or been taken prisoners of war; and (ii) Weapon ban/limiting treaties—limiting the means and methods of warfare which could be used by the adversaries. The present-day rules of IHL are contained in nearly 50 conventions or treaties dealing with matters ranging from the prohibition on the use of certain weapons which cause indiscriminate damage and cause unnecessary suffering, to those that deal with means and methods of warfare.

[4] Hoffman Frank G., "Examining Complex Forms of Conflict: Grey Zone and Hybrid Challenges," *PRISM*, 7, No. 4, (2018), 31-47.

[5] The Grey Zone, "The US Special Operations Command," (9 September 2015), 1.

[6] Morris Lyle J., Michael J. Mazarr, Jeffrey W. Hornung, et.al, *Gaining Competitive Advantage in the Gray Zone: Response Options for Coercive Aggression Below the Threshold of Major War*, (RAND Corporation, 2019) 8-11.

[7] Elizabeth G. Troeder Elizabeth G., A Whole of Government Approach to Grey Zone Warfare, Strategic Studies Institute, (US Army War College, 2019), 38.

[8] In the future, "fake news" put together with the aid of artificial intelligence will be so realistic that even the best-resourced and most professional news organisation will not be able to make the difference between the real and the made-up news. This news can spread across social media in nanoseconds, disseminating information that would undermine the entire democratic institution.

[9] Carment David and Dani Belo, "War's Future: The Risks and Rewards of Grey-Zone Conflict and Hybrid Warfare," (Canadian Global Affairs Institute, October 2018), 15.

[10] For instance, in the recent past, the Chinese civilian fishing boats have caused near-collisions with US military vessels in the South China Sea, off the coast of Chinese man-made islands. The nexus between these agents and the Chinese government is difficult to prove, eluding the traditional law of state responsibility. International law or IHL cannot hold China accountable.

[11] Sun Tzu, *The Art of War* (New York: Fall River Press, 2014), 92.

[12] Kittrie Orde F., *Lawfare: Law as a Weapon of War*, (New York: Oxford University Press, 2016), 172.

[13] Article 37 of the 1977 Additional Protocol I prohibit "perfidy" and defines it as an acts inviting the confidence of an adversary to lead him to believe that he is entitled to, or is obliged to accord, protection under the rules of international law applicable in armed conflict, with intent to betray that confidence.

[14] Fitton Oliver, "Cyber Operations and Gray Zones: Challenges for NATO," *Connections*, 15(2), (2016), 109-119.

[15] Article 51 of the United Nations Charter states, "Nothing in the present Char-ter shall impair the inherent right of individual or collective self-defense if an armed attack occurs against a Member of the United Nations until the Security Council has taken measures necessary to maintain international peace and security."